# INTRODUCTION TO PSYCHOLOGY AND HUMAN NATURE

A BOOK FOR REFEREES AND OTHER SPORTS OFFICIALS

Dubravka Martinović

Graphical designer and cover illustrator:
Caotica (Anamarija Montak) www.caotica.co

Proofreading: SINONIM d.o.o.

*To all who have desire for knowledge*

# Content

# Acknowledgement

I would like to thank the City of Umag, my home town, for helping to fund the process of editing and graphic design for this book. As a city of sports, Umag has truly recognized the value of this book.

Special THANKS to all my friends from the sports officiating world who have allowed me to get to know their profession and its requirements first-hand. Collaboration with you over the past few years has helped me become a better sports psychologist and grow as a professional. I have gained a lot of experience and knowledge, which are priceless and unique. Without you, I would probably never have come to the idea to write such a book. Therefore, referees and referee instructors, thank you for inspiring me to write this book.

# Introduction

This book was written primarily for **referees, umpires, and other sports officials**, but also for all those who would like to know more about the basic psychology principles. It integrates theoretical principles, research findings, everyday life examples, and reflective questions.

The aim of this book is to provide you with some information about psychology and human nature – motivation, emotions, behavior, and personality – the topics you are dealing with in your everyday life and in every game you are officiating.

I truly believe that it would be useful for referees to have knowledge about the nature of human behavior, motivation, and emotions. In some ways it could help you better understand why people behave like they do, how to recognize emotional expressions, and what are personality types and their traits.

If you want to gain insight into motivation and why people react and behave as they do in some situations, this book may help you to better understand and prepare for those situations during the game.

This book is just a modest attempt to introduce you to this interesting scientific and multifaceted academic discipline – psychology.

**Reflective question:**

Ask yourself why knowing more about psychology and human nature could benefit you as a referee?

Each chapter presents one of the following topics:

- Game control aspects
- Motivation
- Emotions
- Behavior
- Personality

# Chapter 1

## GAME CONTROL ASPECTS

Recognizing and understanding people's motivations, such as striving for achievement and power, emotions like anger and frustration, and misbehavior applies not just to your relationships with others but also to your relationship with yourself. This is a part of yourself that has an enormous power over your life.

Your relationships, your work, your life can be determined by your motivation, emotions, and behavior. Incentives and feelings can motivate us to do extraordinary things, yet we know less about our emotions and behavior than about the brand of our clothing, new mobile gadgets or other people's lives.

*"The more you know yourself,*
*the more patience you have for what*
*you see in others."*
(Erik Erikson)

Learning about the basics of motivation, emotions, and behavior can improve your ability to recognize, understand, and know how to deal with some emotional reactions from players, coaches, and other participants. It could also help you to become aware, to understand, and to control your emotional reactions, body language, behavior, and all the motivation behind it.

Understanding facial expressions, body language, and behavior may help you better understand what players and coaches actually feel (and what they want people to think they feel) when protesting, complaining, and misbehaving. Understanding the complexity of emotional experience and behavioral reactions could be crucial for your performance and game control.

During the game, it is important to successfully manage the behavior of many people on the court (including your own). Improving your knowledge of human nature can improve your officiating, game management, and game control. It could help you to better prepare for stressful conflict situations during the game, and resolve them more successfully. In specific situations during the game – for instance when communicating with players and coaches, when giving a warning, when resolving a conflict, when trying to find a solution with your fellow officials, etc., your knowledge of human nature could be very beneficial.

When you prepare yourself for a new season, and even for a new game, it is recommended to remind yourself of the following – *"What is my role as a referee? What are my tasks and my responsibilities during the game?"*

According to the DOT*, referees' main tasks are to:

- *Observe the actions of participants at sporting events to regulate competition and detect interactions of the rules.*
- *Resolve claims of rule interactions, or complaints lodged by participants, and assess penalties based on established regulations.*

In addition, to better understand your role as a referee, you should also think and consider the roles and goals of the participants you are officiating during the game (and whole season). What are the roles, tasks, and goals of the athletes, players, and coaches during the game? Here is an example of a comparison.

Table 1. *Tasks of the main participants during the game*

| **DURING THE GAME** | | |
|---|---|---|
| **Player's tasks** | **Coach's tasks** | **My (referee's) tasks** |
| Play according to the tactics<br>Play according to the situation<br>Perform successfully<br>Make the best possible decisions to win in every situation<br>Perform better than the opponent<br>... | Lead the team<br>Propose tactics and actions<br>Advise the players<br>Make the best possible decisions for the team<br>Lead the team better than the opponent<br>... | Regulate the competition according to the rules<br>Resolve conflict situations<br>Stay focused for better decisions<br>Be objective and precise<br>Have courage for decisions and sanctions<br>... |

*Dictionary of Occupational Titles, CODE:34058L, Referees, umpires, and other sports officials.

Table 2. *Goals of the main participants during the game*

| Player's goals | Coach's goals | My (referee's) goal |
|---|---|---|
| Win the game<br>Have good statistics<br>... | Win the game<br>Progress towards the team's seasonal goal<br>... | Establish game control<br>... |

In this example, the main task for players and coaches is to 'win' in each situation during the game, to be better than the opponent in every moment, and eventually to win the game. On the other hand, the referees' main task is to keep this competition 'under control', professionally, objectively, and according to the rules of their sport.

As can be seen from the example, the referees' role and responsibilities during the game differ from those of coaches and players in one important and significant way – **they want to win the game; referees have to keep that competition fair and under control.**

If someone is competing against another, this can lead to many emotions and behavioral patterns occurring in different situations. Competition can awaken many emotions among participants – anger, frustration, joy, excitement, shame, pride, sadness, etc. It can give rise to many kinds of misbehavior and undesirable reactions from players, coaches, spectators, etc.

Therefore, it will be beneficial to prepare yourself for one of the main psychological characteristics of competition – the occurrence and awakening of emotions and behavior.

When preparing for the game, you should ask yourself: *"What emotions and behavior could occur during this game? How can they effect the game flow? How can I resolve them according to the rules? How can I prepare myself better to stay focused? How to be objective and regain self-control when these situations occur? How will I keep the game and its events under control?"*

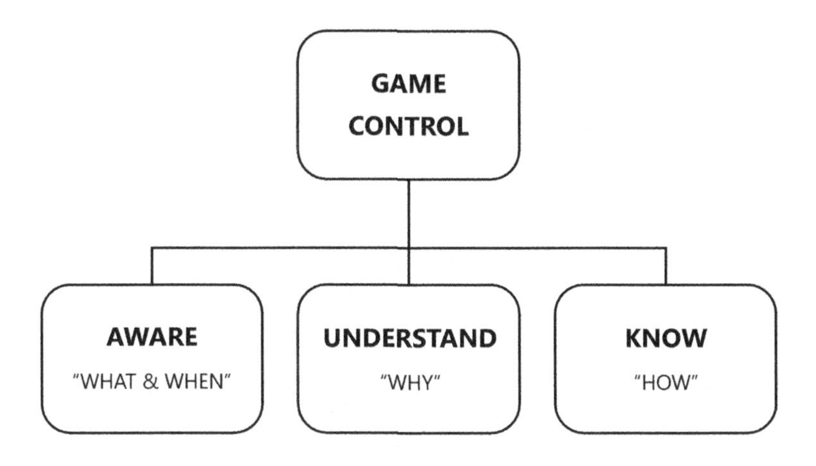


*Figure 1.* Game control aspects

To establish game control, first, the referee needs to be aware and recognize "**what is going on**". Second, when the referee is aware of the situation, he or she has to understand "**why this is happening**", what is the reason behind it. And third, the referee needs to know "**how to resolve it**". What tools, skills, and knowledge does the referee have to resolve the situation professionally under the requirements of the rules?

EXAMPLE (basketball): *You see a coach starting to protest about a decision you made (no call) in the last few minutes of the game. He starts to expressively complain, waving his arms and making inappropriate gestures. You understand that this reaction is a result of the coach's desire to win the game. It is a result of his or her team losing by 3 points in the last 2 minutes of the game. Now, you need to regain self-control (to not be 'eaten' by the coach's emotion), find the appropriate tool or method to handle it in a professional and successful way.*

EXAMPLE (various sports): *Recognize the attempt of two players to provoke a possible 'big fight' situation (they push each other stealthily and sneakily with hands). You understand that this is the way to resolve a conflict from a previous situation your colleague did not see (or call) when one pinched the other behind his back. You also understand that if you do not prevent this, it could even escalate to a bigger fight, between many players. You know that this situation needs to be resolved by communication, warning, or a penalty (or an even stronger sanction).*

It is important to understand the experience of emotions and the motivation behind a certain behavior (e.g. complaining). By understanding the importance of reading the emotional reactions and motivation behind someone's behavior, the referee can anticipate and even prevent some situations from developing further to the point where they can escalate or 'explode'.

The ability to identify emotions on time can improve referees' communication with players and coaches in a variety of situations. It could also help them to manage their own emotional responses before approaching those of others.

When talking about **self-control** and remaining calm even in a conflict situation, it is useful to also become aware of the impressions you give to your various 'audiences' – players, coaches, colleagues, spectators, etc., of your own ways of thinking, feeling, and behaving. The awareness of the bodily sensations involved in emotion is really important. You can use it as an alarm to start with self-control.

The more capable you become in recognizing the complexities of emotional expressions and motivation under certain behavior, the more you will understand yourself and others and have more experience in regulating it.

**Reflective questions:**

In which situations do I usually become emotional during the game?

Am I aware of those feelings? How do I usually cope with them?

Remember this: The only thing we can have under control is ourselves and ourselves only. You can control the way you prepare, the effort you put in, the attitude you present, your emotional reactions, behavior and thoughts, and by having those 'under control' you get closer to establishing 'game control'.

# Chapter 2

## MOTIVATION

**What motivates us to act in certain ways? Why do we do the things we do? What is the motivation behind the choices people make?**

The term motivation comes from the Latin word *movere*, meaning "to move". Motivation is, therefore, a force that directs our behavior to take some action and move toward the desired goal. It includes energy, action, direction, persistence, and determination.

The motivational process usually goes through four phases:

1) A need or goal we want to satisfy (e.g. *hunger and food*)
2) A drive or action that will lead us toward what we want (e.g. *preparing a meal*)
3) Reduction of the need or achievement of the goal (e.g. *eating*)
4) The feeling of satisfaction (e.g. *feeling full*)

*Figure 2.* Motivational process (Musek, 2005)

EXAMPLE: *At the beginning of the season, you want to pass the officiating rules test to renew your officiating license (goal). You prepare a few weeks before by reading the rule book, watching some videos of rule explanations, consulting with your peers, a mentor or national instructor, etc. (taking actions). After completing the test you get the results, and you have passed it with 97% accuracy (achievement). You feel proud, happy, competent, and prepared (satisfaction).*

# THEORIES OF MOTIVATION

More about motivation and its principles is explained through various theories, some of which are presented in this text. Psychologists explain motivation in different ways through different theories. Here presented are only a few of them.

## DRIVE-REDUCTION THEORY

This theory emerged from the work of experimental psychologist Clark Hull (1943), who traced motives back to basic physiological and psychological needs. According to Hull, the thing that motivates us starts with a need that leads to a drive. When the organism is deprived of something it needs or wants (e.g. food or water), it becomes tense and engages in some activity (e.g. seeks for food or water). A need results from a lack of something useful or desirable and produces a drive to achieve it.

EXAMPLE: *Hunger drives us to eat, curiosity drives us to find something out, ambition drives us to achieve something more, and tiredness drives us to rest.*

*Biological needs drive an organism to act, and the organism strives to maintain homeostasis. Homeostasis is the tendency of the body to return to or maintain a balanced state.*

Primary needs have a physiological basis and include the needs for air, food, water, and sex. Secondary needs are derived from primary needs and relate to psychological satisfaction of physiological desires but also to psychological motives, such as achievement and affiliation (Deckers, 2018).

# INCENTIVE THEORY

This theory emphasizes the role of the environment in motivating behavior (Kasschau, 2003). Incentives are reinforcers, rewards, or goals we want to accomplish and achieve. We engage in certain behaviors because we are motivated by positive incentives such as praise, money, or recognition. Two people may act in different ways in the same situation based entirely on the types of incentives that are available to them at that time. You can probably think of many different situations where your behavior was directly influenced by the promise of a reward or punishment.

While drives motivate us to reduce our needs, incentives motivate us to fulfil them.

EXAMPLE: *Hunger (drive) may cause us to go to the pizzeria, but the incentive for our action is the delicious pizza we like to eat. Sometimes, if our drive (hunger) is too strong, we do not care if our food is not so tasty and delicious, but we eat the first thing we find. However, if our drive (hunger) is weak, our incentive must be strong to take action for it (to prepare a delicious meal).*

The theory proposes that people are pulled toward behaviors that lead to rewards and positive consequences, and pushed away from actions that might lead to sanctions and negative consequences.

A reward is an interesting concept when speaking about the consequences of a certain behavior. Sometimes, the purpose and person behind the reward is more important than the reward itself (Reeve, 2009). For some people, praise from the 'important other' is more significant in one activity than a money bonus from another person in another activity.

*A reward is a thing given in recognition of service, effort, or achievement.*

## SELF-DETERMINATION THEORY

Introduced by the psychologists Edward Deci and Richard Ryan in the 1980s, this theory suggests that people are motivated to grow and change by three innate and universal psychological needs:

- **Competence:** a need to be effective, gain knowledge, and learn different skills. When you feel competent (have skills needed for success), you are more likely to take actions that will help you achieve your goals.

- **Relatedness:** a need to have a close, affectionate relationship. To experience a sense of belonging and attachment with others.

- **Autonomy**: a need to control the choices you make and the actions you take – the course of your life.

The self-determination concept refers to person's ability to make choices and manage their own life. Self-determination allows people to feel that they have control over their motivation, choices, actions, and life (Ryan and Deci, 2000).

The concept of intrinsic motivation, or engaging in activities for the behavior itself, plays an important role in the self-determination theory.

## INTRINSIC AND EXTRINSIC MOTIVATION

**Which motivation is dominant in an individual's behavior, extrinsic or intrinsic? How do internal sources of motivation differ from external sources of motivation?**

We can explain motivation also by looking at forces inside of us, arising from internal factors called intrinsic motivation, and forces outside of us, arising from external factors called extrinsic motivation. Both energize us to move.

**INTRINSIC MOTIVATION** refers to engaging in activities because those activities are personally rewarding or because engaging them fulfills our beliefs or expectations (Kasschau, 2003). It is doing an activity simply for the enjoyment of the activity itself (Ryan and Deci, 2000).

**EXTRINSIC MOTIVATION** refers to engaging in activities to reduce needs or obtain incentives and goal, or external rewards (Kasschau, 2003). It is doing something because it leads to a desirable outcome (Ryan and Deci, 2000).

Needs (physiological, psychological, social) can be both internal and external motives. Also, a behavior that begins for extrinsic reasons can be exhibited for its own sake, that is, for intrinsic reasons.

EXAMPLE: *You may go out to dinner with your friends both because you need to satisfy your hunger (extrinsic motivation) and because you enjoy the taste of the restaurant's food and wish to socialize with your friends (intrinsic motivation). Or: a student who enrolled in a course for one semester because it was required by his university (extrinsic motivation) ends up liking it, and continues to attend it even for the next semester (intrinsic motivation).*

People differ in their motives. Some do more activities that are intrinsically motivated, others do more that are extrinsically motivated. This depends on many things, such as their personality traits, personal values, upbringing, life circumstances, etc. In reality, our motivations are often a mix of both intrinsic and extrinsic factors, and can change over time.

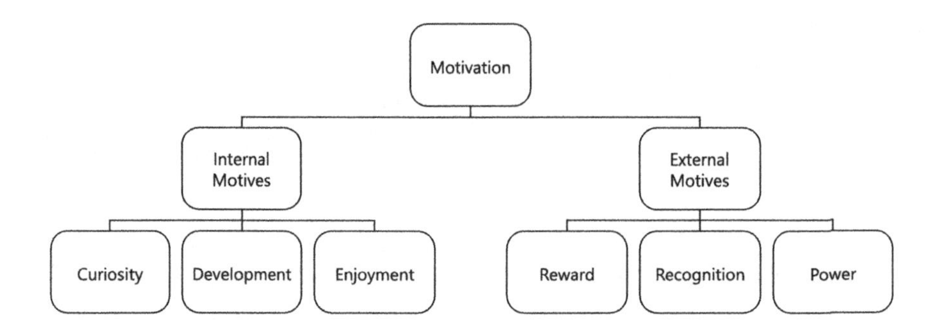


*Figure 3.* An example of internal and external motives for a person

EXAMPLE: *If you are officiating because you love the game, or you wish to excel at this profession, you are following intrinsic motivation. However, if you are officiating because you want to be recognized in society, or you want to earn some money while officiating, you are following extrinsic motivation. In many cases, we engage in activities because of both extrinsic and intrinsic motivations.*

**Reflective questions:**

When amateur athletes become professionals, does money make them enjoy their sport more or less?

Do retired professional athletes still play their sport for fun?

When referees attend the Olympics for the first time, does this achievement make their desire for improvement stop or continue?

When speaking about external motivation, it is important to consider the concept of consequence. **Consequence** is an external regulator of motivation, and involves reinforcers and punishers (Reeve, 2009).

- Reinforcers (e.g. praise), when presented, increase the probability of that behavior in the future.
- Punishers (e.g. speed limit ticket), when presented, decrease the probability of that behavior in the future.

Consequences follow behavior and increase or decrease the persistence of behavior. More about this topic is explained in Chapter 4: Behavior.

Motives can also depend on **social and cultural preferences**, upbringing values, or personality. Some cultural preferences and values can have the capacity to energize and direct a person's behavior. In some cultures, achieving status and power are highly important motives, while in others the experience of doing some activity in itself and the learning process through development are preferable motives.

# NEEDS HIERARCHY THEORY

A very influential theory of motivation was Abraham Maslow's *hierarchy of needs* (1943). He proposed a hierarchy of five innate needs that activate and direct human behavior. The cornerstone of this theory is the proposition that human needs can be organized into different clusters, and he proposed five: physiological, safety, belongingness, esteem, and self-actualization. According to his theory:

- Needs arrange themselves in a hierarchy according to potency, strength, and priority. The lower the need is in the hierarchy, the stronger and more urgently it is felt.
- The lower the need is in the hierarchy, the sooner it appears in life and development.
- The needs in the hierarchy are fulfilled sequentially, from lowest to highest, from the base of the pyramid to its top.
- Because higher needs are less necessary for actual survival, their gratification can be postponed.
- A need does not have to be satisfied fully before the next need in the hierarchy becomes important.

The original Maslow's theory was revised into more extended and elaborated points presenting the hierarchy as split into two distinct sections (Collin et al., 2012):

- **Deficiency needs:** physiological, safety, love and belongingness, and self-esteem
- **Growth needs:** cognitive, aesthetic, and spiritual and psychological fulfillment (self-actualization and self-transcendence)

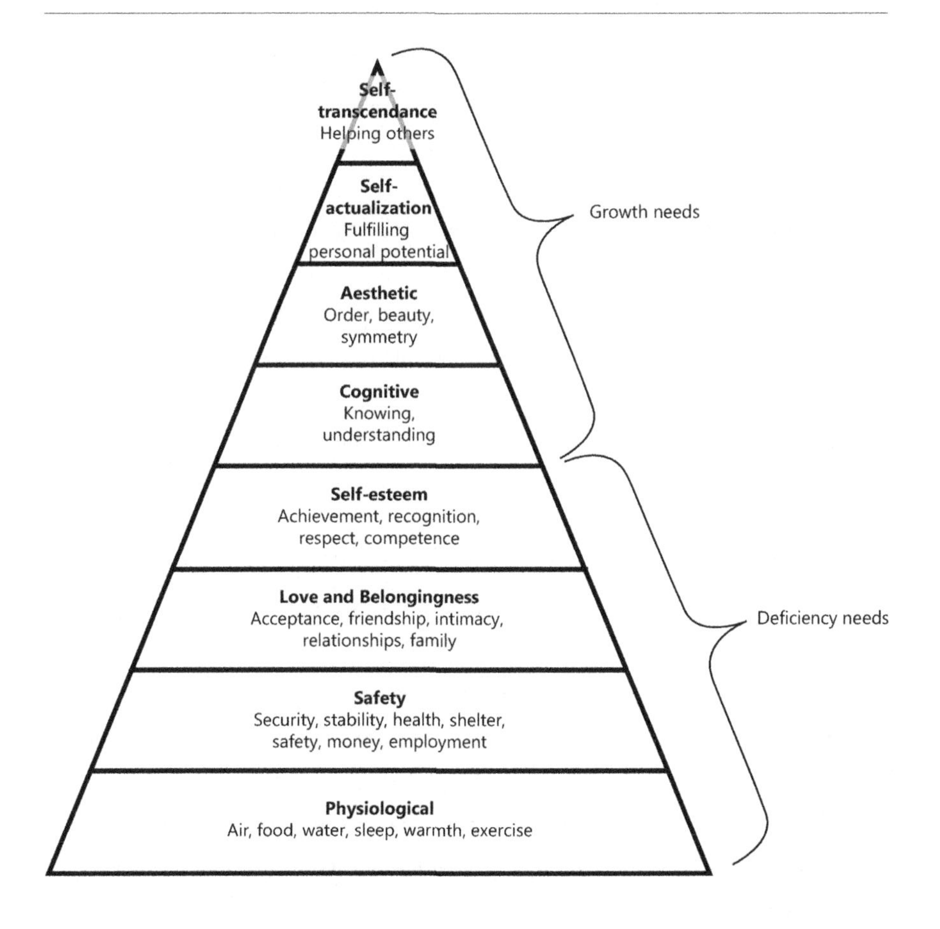


*Figure 4.* Revised Maslow's theory of needs (Source: The Psychology Book: Big Ideas Simply Explained, (ed.) Collin et al., 2012).

Although arranged hierarchically, a specific need can become dominant at any time. A person's stage in life and current circumstances determine what need is the most potent or urgent to satisfy. Growth needs or self-actualization needs provide energy and direction to become what one is capable of becoming.

*"What a man can be, he must be.*
*He must be true to his own nature."*
(Abraham Maslow)

He proposes that each of us has an individual purpose to which we are uniquely suited, and part of the path to fulfillment is to identify and pursue that purpose. If someone is not doing what they are best suited to do in life, it will not matter if all their other needs are fulfilled, he or she will be restless and unsatisfied. Each of us must discover our potential and seek out experiences that will allow us to fulfill it and reach self-actualization.

Maslow (1971) also offered several everyday behaviors for encouraging the motivation for growth and self-actualization:

- **Make growth choices** – see life as a series of choices.
- **Be honest** – take responsibility for your choices and the consequences of those choices.
- **Situationally position yourself for peak experiences** – set up conditions to make peak experiences more likely. Learn what your potential is.
- **Give up defensiveness** – identify defenses and find the courage to give them up.
- **Let the self emerge** – instead of only looking to others to tell you who to become, also listen to your own personal interests and aspirations of who you want to become.
- **Be open to experience** – experience fully, vividly, selflessly with the full concentration and total absorption. Be spontaneous, original, and open to the experience.

*"You will either step forward toward growth*
*or you will step back into safety."*
(Abraham Maslow)

## THREE NEEDS THEORY

Psychologist David McClelland's acquired needs theory (1961) proposes that an individual's specific needs are developed over time and shaped by experience. According to him, motivation is a key component of any performance, but what people say about their motives should not be taken for granted because motivations are largely unconscious. There are three key motivations that drive performance:

**NEED FOR ACHIEVEMENT**: the drive to excel, improve, master, accomplish, overcome obstacles, and live up to a high standard of excellence. Achievement motivates people to constantly seek improvement and ways of doing things better. For them, achievement is more important than material reward. Achievement motivation is guided by two internal sources: the motive to achieve success, and the motive to avoid failure. The motive to achieve is characterized by wanting to do things well and excellent. In contrast, the motive to avoid failure is characterized by the fear and anxiety about failing at a task.

**NEED FOR AFFILIATION**: the drive to create and maintain a warm social relationship, feel loved and accepted by others. This person prefers maintaining good relationships and collaboration over competition and dominance.

**NEED FOR POWER**: the drive to influence and manage other people. A person motivated by power enjoys competition, status recognition, winning arguments, and influencing others. Strivings are often centered around a need for dominance, reputation, status, or position. They always prefer taking leadership roles and positions. The need for power can be expressed in many ways – aggressive or antisocial behavior, or prosocial actions like providing help or advice.

While everyone has all three motivations, he maintained that one would be dominant, directing a person's behavior, and shaping the person's performance.

EXAMPLE: *A successful employee with a high need for affiliation and low need for power begins to perform poorly after being promoted to a manager. He fails to be more directive when setting goals and giving assignments to others.*

EXAMPLE: *If a very good crew chief with a high need for power becomes umpire 1 (basketball), or a head referee is assigned as a line referee (football), he or she may start to feel frustrated, perform badly and/or even sabotage the crew's performance.*

People with a high need for power are more likely to experience frustration (and even aggression) when they feel powerless or when they lose a power position.

*"A great leader makes people feel that they are the cause, not the pawns, of the system."*
(David McClelland)

Psychologist David Winter in his book *The Power Motive* (1973) described the need for power as a desire to have "impact, control, or influence over another person, group, or the world at large".

- **"Impact"** allows power-needing individuals to establish power.
- **"Control"** allows power-needing individuals to maintain power.
- **"Influence"** allows power-needing individuals to expand or restore power.

They strive for leadership and recognition in groups, experience frequent impulses of aggression, prefer influential occupations, and collect prestige possessions (Deckers, 2018; Reeve, 2015).

**Reflective questions:**

Do you think that people in influential positions usually abuse their power more than they should?

Do you think that in occupations involving a legitimate right and duty to direct others' behavior (such as police officers, sports officials, judges, etc.) people use this right to feel more dominant over others, or to regulate their behavior in a strictly professional way?

How do you see your motivation for officiating – as an achievement motive, as a self-actualization motive, as a power motive, or other motive(s)?

# Chapter 3

## EMOTIONS

**What are emotions? How do we express them? Why do they appear? Why do we become emotional when we do?**

Emotions are subjective feelings provoked by real or imagined objects or events that have high significance to the individual. They are a set of complex reactions to stimuli involving subjective feelings, physiological arousal, and observable behavior (Kasschau, 2003).

There are hundreds of emotions, along with their blends, variations, and mutations. There are many more subtleties of emotions than we have words for (Goleman, 2009).

We can explain emotions also as a particular kind of mental experience (Robinson, 2009), which is:

- Strongly motivated by some subjective qualities, like pleasure or pain
- Response to some event or object that is either real or imagined
- Cause, trigger, or motive of a particular behavior

Emotions should have three main aspects (Kasschau, 2003):

- **Physical aspect** – has to do with how an emotion affects the physical arousal of an individual. This level of arousal directs the body on how to respond to the experienced emotion.
- **Behavioral aspect** – it refers to the outward expression of the emotion, such as body language, hand gestures, and the tone of voice.
- **Cognitive aspect** – concerns how we think about or interpret a situation which affects our emotions.

## WHAT CAUSES AN EMOTION?

Cognitive and biological processes in significant situational events are causes of emotional experience. Feelings, sense of purpose, bodily arousal and social expressiveness are products of the emotional process of experiencing one event (Reeve, 2009).

We have **two synchronous systems** that activate and regulate emotions. One system is an innate, spontaneous, physiological system that reacts involuntarily to emotional stimuli. The second system is an experience-based cognitive system that reacts interpretively and socially. Together, the biological and cognitive systems combine to provide a highly adaptive, two-system emotion mechanism (Reeve, 2009).

Emotions derive from physiological changes in our brain and body. The brain recognizes the physiological changes and, as a result of the cognitive process, our thoughts, and interpretations, we experience a situation, we interpret a situation, and we feel emotion. In both ways, we demonstrate observable behavior.

When an event triggers automatic fear reactions or is perceived as stressful, physiological reactions in the body are triggered at the biological level. Such feelings as "makes my heart race" and "choked up with rage" or "ready to vomit" are experienced psychologically in emotional states that involve bodily changes (Mischel, Shoda and Ayduk, 2008).

Dutch psychologist Nico Frijida (2006) explained emotions as an outcome of the process of evaluating the world in terms of a person's concerns. Emotions arise in response to events that are important to the individual's goals, motives, concerns. Every **emotion hides a concern**. A concern is what gives a particular event its emotional meaning. He argues that emotions arise because events are appraised by people as favorable or harmful to their own interests (Frijida, 2006).

Emotions sometimes begin so quickly that we are not even aware of what triggers an emotion in our mind at a given moment. Sometimes we do not have much control over why we become emotional, but it is possible to become aware of the triggers that usually activate certain emotions and how we behave after that (Ekman and Freisen, 2003).

On the other hand, sometimes emotions arise as the result of **how we cognitively evaluate situations, activities, or ourselves**. They inform the individual of how a situation has been evaluated. Therefore, they can influence our thinking, cognitive judgments, and decisions (Deckers, 2018).

*"People and things do not upset us.*
*Rather, we upset ourselves by believing*
*that they can upset us."*
(Albert Ellis)

## IRRATIONAL BELIEFS AND EMOTIONS

One of the most influential psychologists in history, Dr. Albert Ellis, based his work on how an individual's beliefs strongly affect their emotional functioning and behaviors. He called them "irrational beliefs" because they are illogical, distorted thoughts and ideas. According to Ellis (1995), irrational beliefs are the source of psychological distress. They make people feel depressed, anxious, and angry and lead to self-defeating behaviors. People do not get emotionally disturbed by circumstances, but by how they construct their views of these circumstances through their beliefs about the world, themselves, and others.

He identifies three common irrational beliefs regarding demands about the self, other people, or the world. These beliefs include the following thoughts (Ellis, 2003):

1) "**I must be competent, adequate, achieving, and lovable at all times, or else I am an incompetent worthless person.**" This belief usually leads to feelings of anxiety, panic, depression, despair, and worthlessness.

2) "**Other significant people in my life must treat me kindly and fairly at all times or else I can't stand it, and they are bad, rotten, and evil persons who should be severely blamed, damned, and vindictively punished for their treatment of me.**" This leads to feelings of anger, rage, fury.

3) "**Things and conditions absolutely must be the way I want them to be and must never be too difficult or frustrating. Otherwise, life is awful, terrible, horrible, catastrophic and unbearable.**" This leads to frustration, self-pity, anger, depression, procrastination, and avoidance.

Many times, situations are interpreted as a threat or challenge. Perceiving situations as threatening can lead to self-doubt, experiencing emotions such as fear, anxiety, or shame. Perceiving a situation as challenging can awaken self-confidence, expectancy, and pride.

EXAMPLE: *You receive a nomination to officiate one of the play-off games. If you start to interpret this as a threatening situation (for instance: "Oh, this game is so important. I cannot make any mistakes or else everyone will think I am a bad referee."), you will experience fear, anxiety, and self-doubt, which could eventually result in poor performance (poor officiating). On the other hand, you can interpret that as challenging (for instance: "This is what I have been preparing for. I officiated really great during the season, and this is a reward of my performance. I will do my best.") and see it as an opportunity to excel even more. You will probably feel proud, confident, and ready, which could eventually lead to better performance (successful officiating).*

Our subjective interpretation of objective events can have an influence on how we feel and behave – how we experience them.

Also, what we think about how other people perceive us can give rise to many emotions. Shame, guilt, embarrassment, and pride are self-conscious emotions that result from how we think other people are evaluating us (Deckers, 2018).

**Reflective questions:**

How do you usually interpret situations? As a threat or as a challenge?

Are you aware of the importance of the situational context in which emotions appear?

Do you feel shame or embarrassment when you make a mistake during the game?

# CULTURAL CONTEXT

All of us are born with the capacity for emotion and certain basic forms of expression, but when, where, and how we express different feelings depend in large part on learning and social environment, the culture we were raised in (Kasschau, 2003). Basic emotions are universal (regardless of race, culture, or language) and have clearly identifiable facial expressions, but there are cultural differences in when these expressions are shown and how intensively (Ekman and Friesen, 2003).

In social contexts, we share our emotional experiences in various ways – mimicry, gestures, facial expressions, body language, words we use, things we say, actions we take. People in various cultures differ in what they have been taught about managing or controlling their expressions of emotion. A culture, in particular ways, molds its members to experience and express emotions and reactions, and therefore many emotional expressions are socially, rather than biologically, motivated and shaped.

There are social conventions and cultural rules about which emotions you can show, for instance *"boys do not cry or look afraid"*, *"girls should not be aggressive and express anger"*, *"a child should be taught never to look angrily at his or her father"*, or *"never show sadness when disappointed"*. These display rules, whether cultural (shared by most people) or personal, individual ones, are usually so well-learned, and learned so early, that the control of the facial expression they dictate is done automatically without thinking or awareness (Ekman and Freisen, 2003).

EXAMPLE: *In some cultures, it is inappropriate to feel anger or even pride. In other cultures, shame and modesty are considered to be positive emotions.*

Successful adaptation in a new environment implies the ability to feel and express all emotions in appropriate settings. The society usually dictates that "*there is a time and a place for everything*", even for emotions and their expression. All emotions can be adaptive within human society, but it is important to sort out the specific circumstances in which emotions can sometimes fail in their adaptive task (Plutchik, 2001).

## ARE EMOTIONS USEFUL OR HARMFUL?

Emotions respond to a particular situation directing out attention and channeling our behavior to where it is needed, to circumstances we need to face. They can be functional, purposive, and adoptive organizers of behavior (Reeve, 2009).

According to psychologist Robert Plutchik (1980), emotions serve at least eight distinct purposes: protection, destruction, reproduction, reunion, affiliation, rejection, exploration, and orientation.

Fear does protect us; we can save our lives because we are able to respond to threats of harm protectively, without thought. Disgust reactions make us cautious about indulging in activities that might be toxic for us. Sadness and despair over loss may bring help from others. Even anger, an emotion most people would like to turn off, can be sometimes useful for us; it can motivate us to try to change the world, to bring social justice, to fight for human rights (Ekman and Freisen, 2003).

Anger can even be productive when it energizes vigor, strength, and endurance in our efforts to cope productively as we change the world around us into what it should be (Reeve, 2009).

Emotions also serve social functions (Izard, 1989; Keltner and Haidt, 1999; Manstead, 1991; in Reeve, 2009):

- Influence how others interact with us
- Invite and facilitate social interaction
- Create, maintain, and dissolve relationships

In the context of social interaction, emotional expression nonverbally communicates to prepare us for what one's upcoming behavior is likely to be, in ways of (Ekman, 1993; Reeve, 2009):

- Informing – *"This is how I feel"*
- Warning – *"This is what I am about to do"*
- Directing – *"This is what I want to do"*

But emotions are not always helpful, and it is important to regulate them to help us benefit from what is useful about them and to avoid what is not useful. People often must regulate their affects, moods, impulses, and responses (Suri and Gross, 2016).

Ekman and Freisen (2003) state that, generally, people control their emotions because of:

- Culturally displayed rules
- Upbringing and personal rules and values
- Vocational requirement
- Need of the moment

**Reflective questions:**

Do you think sports officiating is a profession that requires efficient self-regulation in emotional control?

Can you recognize 'the need of the moment' to control your emotions during the game?

## EMOTION IS A COMPLEX CHAIN

Human emotions are best viewed through an evolutionary lens, as adaptations triggered by the challenges of survival and reproduction that are part of every organism's existence (Plutchik, 2001).

According to psychologist Robert Plutchik (1980), emotion is a complex chain of loosely connected events that begins with a stimulus and includes feelings, psychological changes, impulses to action and specific, goal-directed behavior. They are responses to significant situations and often motivate actions.

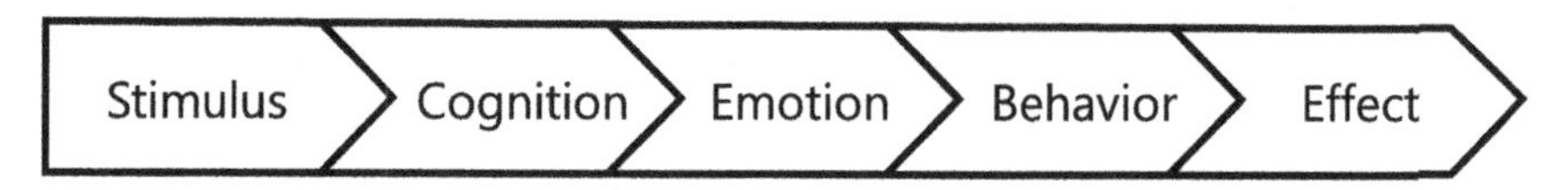


*Figure 5.* Emotion as a complex chain (Source: Plutchik, 2001)

Table 3. *Process of emotions according to Plutchik (2001)*

| Stimulus situation | Cognition | Emotion | Emotional behavior | Effect |
|---|---|---|---|---|
| Threat | "danger" | Fear | Escape | Safety |
| Obstacle | "enemy" | Anger | Attack | Destruction |
| Gain | "possess" | Joy | Retain | Gain resource |
| Loss | "abandonment" | Sadness | Cry | Reattach |
| Membership | "friend" | Acceptance | Groom | Support |
| Distasteful | "poison" | Disgust | Vomit | Eject |
| New territory | "examine" | Expectancy | Map | Knowledge |
| Unexpected | "what is it?" | Surprise | Stop | Time to orient |

<u>EXAMPLE:</u> *During the game, a coach may show anger with gestures of protest, including inappropriate words. He feels that your decision is an 'obstacle' for him to win the game. Through behavior (verbal attack), the coach is trying to 'destroy' your decision and your credibility.*

A three-dimensional circumplex model of emotions was also proposed by Robert Plutchik in 1958. He suggested that the eight primary emotions can be conceptualized and presented as a color wheel (Figure 6.). The eight sectors are designed to indicate that there are eight primary emotions arranged as four pairs of opposites.

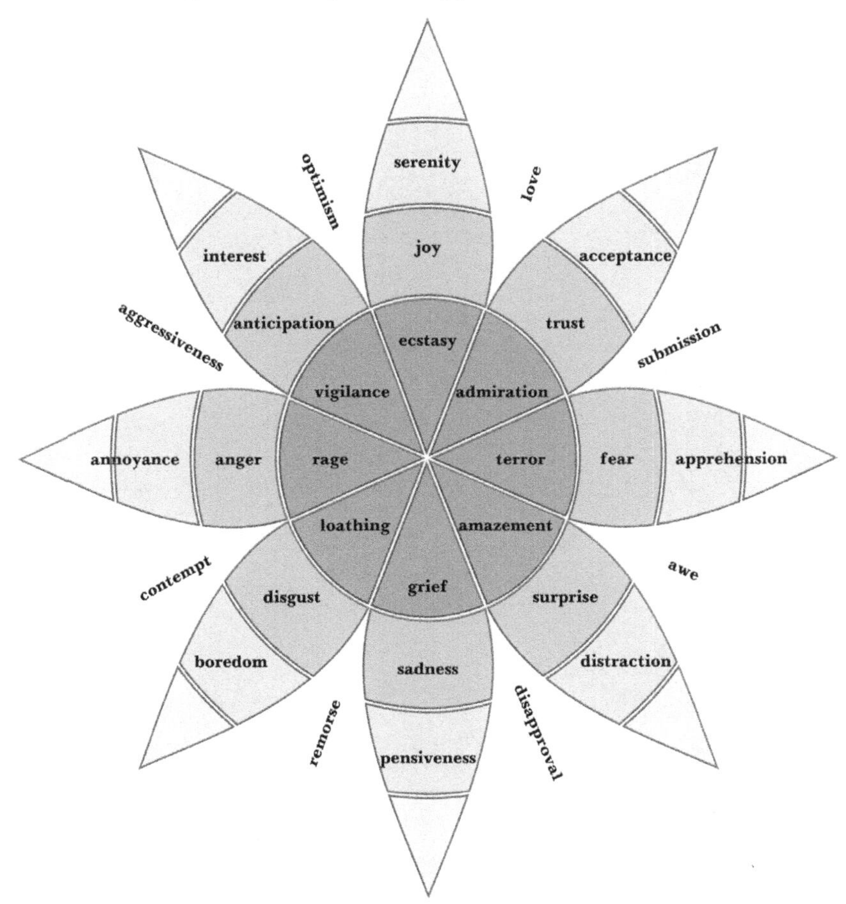


*Figure 6.* Three-dimensional circumplex model of emotions (Source: Plutchik, 2001)

As we can see, he placed similar emotions close together and opposite ones 180 degrees apart (Plutchik, 2001):

- *joy* versus *sadness*
- *anger* versus *fear*
- *acceptance* versus *disgust*
- *surprise* versus *expectancy*

The emotions in the blank spaces are the primary dyads or combinations of two of the primary emotions, such as: love=(joy+trust), contempt=(disgust+anger).

## DIFFERENCE BETWEEN EMOTION AND MOOD

Emotions arise in response to a specific event, motivate specific behaviors and last seconds or perhaps minutes. Moods are affect states that can last over a longer period of time (for hours or even days) (Ekman and Freisen, 2003).

Emotions mostly influence behavior and direct specific courses of action. Moods, however, mostly influence cognition and direct what the person thinks about (Reeve, 2009). Moods like anxiety and depression can last for days, weeks, months or even longer. They can influence the quality of one's well-being and life in general, often leading to problems in everyday functioning and social relationships.

Mood also can influence our behavior and directions of our attention, and vice versa – what we focus our attention on and the consequences of our behavior can have implications to our mood (Pervin, 2003).

A mood can also activate specific emotions; for example, when we are irritable, we are seeking an opportunity to become angry; we interpret the world in a way that permits, or even requires us to become angry (Ekman and Freisen, 2003).

## BASIC EMOTIONS

Are you familiar with the award-winning TV series *Lie to Me*, where actor Tim Roth plays a psychologist who can detect deception from facial micro-expressions in people (that is, whether they are lying or telling the truth)? This show was inspired by the work and research of psychologist and Professor Emeritus Dr. Paul Ekman. He is a pioneer in the study of emotions and their relation to facial expressions and has gained a reputation as the best human lie detector. He has created an "atlas of emotions" with more than ten thousand facial expressions.

Having traveled all around the world, he found that people from different countries could interpret the facial expressions of basic emotions, which suggests that facial expressions are universal products of human evolution (Ekman and Freisen, 2003; Ekman, 2003).

*"Without knowing a person's culture or a language, you can tell whether he or she is amused or infuriated just by looking at a person's face.*
(Paul Ekman)

There are many different types of emotions that people are capable of experiencing, and Ekman describes six basic, universal emotions – ANGER, DISGUST, FEAR, HAPPINESS, SADNESS, AND SURPRISE. He notes that the facial expressions linked to these emotions are involuntary – we react automatically to things that trigger these emotional responses, and this reaction often happens before our conscious mind has time to register the causes of that emotion.

When looking at someone, you gather information about their emotional state and feelings from many sources (Ekman and Freisen, 2003):

- Facial expressions
- Body posture
- Muscle movements
- Sound of voice
- Words used
- Rhythm of speech

Each one of these sources can tell you something about emotions, especially the face and the voice (Ekman, 2003). The face is, nevertheless, of more importance than words for transmitting information about emotion.

According to Eckman (2003), emotions are shown primarily in the face, not in the body. **The body instead shows how people are coping with emotion.** There is no specific body movement pattern that always signals anger or fear, but there are facial patterns specific to each emotion. If someone is angry, their body may show how they are coping with anger. They may be tense and constrained (tight muscular tension in arms and legs, stiff posture). They may be withdrawing (a particular retreated position). There may be a verbal attack (certain types of hand movements along with words) or the likelihood of a physical attack (posture, orientation, hand movements). However, any of these movements can occur just as well when the person is afraid as when they are angry (Ekman and Freisen, 2003).

In a state of fear, when hands begin to tremble, it is much easier to do something with them – make a fist or fold them – then just let them tremble. But when lips are tightening and stretching, and the eye brows are pulled up in fear, it is very hard to keep a still face (Ekman, 1992).

Words, on the other hand, are easy to rehearse, again and again. Speakers have an immediate feedback to what they say, and they are able to modify and tune their message. Body movements are also a good source of clues as to how someone is feeling. They can reveal not just how someone copes with emotion, but also how to interpret the situation, and what a person's attitudes, interpersonal orientations, etc. might be (Ekman, 1992; Ekman and Friesen, 2003).

Here are presented six basic emotions mainly described by Paul Ekman in his books *Telling Lies* (1992), *Unmasking the Face* (2003), and *Emotions Revealed* (2003):

## SURPRISE

Surprise is the briefest emotion. It arises as the response to something unexpected. You can never be surprised for a long time.

We are usually familiar with the appearance of surprise in combination with elements of a second emotion, such as fear, happiness, sadness, or even anger.

Surprise is characterized by:

- Facial expressions such as raising the eyebrows, widening the eyes, and opening the mouth (the jaw drops open)
  ... But also by:
- Physical responses such as freezing, stepping back, placing a hand on the mouth
- Verbal reactions such as yelling, screaming, gasping or feeling stunned and speechless.

## FEAR

Fear is an emotional reaction that arises from a person's interpretation that the situation they face is dangerous and a threat to one's life or well-being (Revee, 2009). The harm may be physical or psychological, or both. It may involve both physical pain and psychological suffering (Ekman and Freisen, 2003).

You can fear both real and imagined threats of harm. The fear of danger and the anticipation of even physical pain can often be more miserable than the pain itself.

<u>EXAMPLE:</u> *You may experience a more intense fear when preparing to go to the dentist than when you actually get there.*

Fear differs from surprise in three important ways. Fear is a terrible experience, and surprise is not. Surprise is not necessarily pleasant or unpleasant, but even mild fear is unpleasant. Strong fear – terror – is probably the most traumatic of all emotions. It is accompanied by many changes in the body (pale skin, cold sweat, rapid breathing, heart pounding, trembling hands, frozen posture, etc.).

The second way fear differs from surprise is that you can be afraid of something familiar that you know full well is going to happen. When fear is felt suddenly, when there is no anticipation of danger, but the fear is simultaneous with harm, the experience may be tinged with surprise. Thus, in many of these sudden experiences, you could experience a blend of surprise and fear.

A third way in which fear differs from surprise is in its duration. Surprise is the briefest emotion, but, unfortunately, fear is not. Surprise always has a short duration. Fear can last much longer. How intense the experience of fear is depends upon the event or your appraisal of the event.

Fear may be followed by any of the other emotions, or by no emotion at all. You may become angry, sad, or even happy that it is over.

Not everyone experiences fear in the same way. Some people can experience fear in situations that others can find not frightening at all. It depends on their interpretation of the situation. Some people can interpret new situations mainly as threatening and feel fear, whereas others can interpret them as challenging and not experience fear at all.

Expressions of fear can include:

- Facial expressions of wide-open eyes with the eyebrows raised and drawn together, and open jaw with chin drawn back
- Behavior such as shaking, hiding, or even attacking the source of fear
- Physiological reactions such as rapid breathing and a fast heartbeat, or even crying

**Reflective question:**

When you become afraid, do you get aggressive, withdrawn, or thoughtful?

## DISGUST

Disgust is a feeling of aversion and involves getting rid of or getting away from a contaminated, deteriorated, or spoiled object. It can be the body's way of avoiding things that may carry transmittable diseases. Taste, smell, touch, thought, sight, sound, appearance, or even ideas can be disgusting. What is repulsive to people in one culture may be attractive to people in another culture.

**Contempt** is a close relative to disgust, but it differs in some ways. Contempt is only experienced about people or their actions when you observe others engaging in behaviors that you find distasteful, immoral, bad, or evil.

Often, disgust or contempt will be experienced together with anger. You can be angry at someone for being disgusting.
If a person's actions make you disgusted rather than angry, it is usually because they pose no threat; your response is to get away from them rather than to defend yourself or attack them. Disgust is often used to mask anger because in parts of our society there is a taboo against expressing anger.

The most important clues to disgust are manifested in the mouth and the nose. Disgust can be displayed in many ways, including:

- Facial expressions such as wrinkling the nose and raising or curling the upper lip
- Turning away from the object of disgust
- A physical reaction such as vomiting or retching

Contempt
- Tightened lip corner with a bit of a smile, one lip corner slightly raised on one side

## ANGER

Anger arises from restraint, as in the interpretation that one's plans or goals have been interfered with by some barriers, obstacles, or interruptions. It can also arise from a betrayal of trust, receiving unwarranted criticism, a lack of consideration from others, and cumulative annoyances (Fehr et al. 1999; in Reeve, 2009).

Generally, there are four major sources of anger: frustration, physical threat, insult or statement (psychological hurt), and observing someone do something which violates your dearly held moral values.

Anger is the most passionate and probably the most dangerous emotion. When angry, you are more likely to hurt others intentionally; its purpose is to destroy barriers in the environment. Part of the experience of anger is the risk of losing control. Sometimes a person who was angry feels regret about the things they said or did when such loss of control happened. They may say, for instance, *"I know I shouldn't have said that, but I was furious; I've lost my temper."*

Anger varies in intensity and may build gradually, from slight irritation or annoyance to rage or fury. People differ in terms of what makes them angry or what they do when they are angry, as well as in terms of how long it takes them to become angry.

People also differ in how long they remain angry once the provocation has passed. Those whose emotional expression of anger is generally quicker or stronger have a much harder time cooling it off.

Anger is manifested in many ways:

- Facial expressions such as frowning or glaring, eyebrows lowered and drawn together, the eyes have a hard stare and may have a bulging

appearance
- The face may redden, the veins on the forehead and neck may become more apparent
- The tone of voice, speaking gruffly or yelling
- Physiological responses such as sweating or fast breathing
- Aggressive behaviors such as hitting, kicking, or throwing objects

Uncontrolled anger can turn to aggression, abuse, or violence. This is important to observe and recognize during the game because the referee can eventually anticipate and prevent aggressive behavior from turning into uncontrolled violence.

With the ability to identify emotions early on, the referee may be able to deal properly with a variety of situations and have time to manage the emotional responses to their own feelings.

## HAPPINESS

Happiness is the emotional evidence that things are going well (e.g. success, achievement, progress, respect, love). It is the emotion most people strive for and want to experience. If you can, you choose situations in which you will experience happiness. It is a pleasant emotion that is characterized by the feelings of joy, satisfaction, and well-being.

Happiness is a positive emotion. Fear, anger, disgust, and sadness are negative emotions; surprise is neither positive nor negative.

In order to understand the experience of happiness, we need to distinguish it from two closely related states which often occur with happiness – pleasure and excitement. Pleasure is the opposite of the physical sensation of pain. You value, appreciate, and prefer pleasurable sensations. Excitement is the opposite of boredom. You become excited when something arouses your interest.

Smiles, which are part of the facial expression of happiness, often occur when a person is not happy. You smile to mask other emotions or to qualify them. Smiles may also be used to make a tense situation more comfortable. By smiling, you can also cause the other person to smile also because it is hard to resist returning a smile.

Happiness is shown and expressed through:

- Facial expressions such as smiling, the cheeks are raised, with wrinkles going outward from the outer corners of the eyes
- Body language such as relaxed stance
- An upbeat, pleasant tone of voice

## SADNESS

Sadness arises principally from experiences of loss, disappointment, hopelessness, and failure. Anything can make us sad, but most often we are sad about loss. Sadness is a passive, not an active feeling. All people can experience sadness from time to time. We can be sad for a few minutes, but more typically a few hours or even days.

We experience suffering in sadness. It is not the suffering of physical pain; it is the suffering of loss, disappointment, or hopelessness. Sadness can blend with many emotions, but more often with anger and fear.

Sadness can be expressed in many ways, including:

- Facial expressions such as the corners of the lips are down or the lip is trembling, the inner corners of the eyebrows are drawn up and triangulated, the upper eyelid inner corner is raised
- Sorrowful mood, quietness, and lethargy
- Withdrawal from others and isolation
- Crying

## CONTROLLING FACIAL EXPRESSIONS

We do not have much control over our emotional states, but it is possible to make some changes in what triggers them and how we express them – how we interpret the situation and the context in which we are, and even how we behave when we are emotional.

According to Ekman and Freisen (2003), it is easier to monitor your words as you speak than to monitor your facial expressions. People have more practice in lying with words than with their faces, and there are two reasons. First, facial expressions can be extremely rapid, flashing on and off the face in less than a second. With words you can hear yourself speak, managing what you are saying word by word. On the other hand, you can't see your own facial expressions, instead you must rely upon a less accurate source of information about what is going on your face – the feedback from the facial muscles. It is easier to falsify words than facial expressions, which is why facial expressions can be more truthful then words.

If you do not want to be misled, and if you are not dealing with a professional liar, then you need to recognize signs of leakage and deception clues. The four factors (Ekman and Freisen, 2003) must be interpreted in light of the social context in which an expression occurs:

1) Morphology (the particular configuration of the appearance of the face)
2) Timing (how long it takes for it to appear on the face, how long it remains, and how long it takes to disappear)
3) Location (where the expression is placed in relationship to words)
4) Micro-expressions (last less than a second)

**Reflective questions:**

Do you compare people's facial expressions with their body movements, posture, tone of voice?

Do you notice the timing and duration of an expression?

Do you really want to know how the person actually feels, or would you instead prefer to know only what they want you to know?

Are you able to detect falsified expressions intended to fool you, to mislead you about how the person actually feels?

The social context includes other behaviors (body posture, body movement, voice, words) and definition of the situation (Ekman and Freisen, 2003).

Individuals who generally have faster and stronger emotional responses will have a much harder time cooling off, and controlling such emotional behavior will not always work. Even if it doesn't always work, it is important to try and continue. The key is to understand ourselves and others better. By monitoring and analyzing our feelings we are more likely to increase our ability to spot the signs of how others respond emotionally. This can also help us respond to others' emotions and reactions in an appropriate way.

EXAMPLE: *Think of the situations than can awaken emotional reactions in you and the amount of time it takes you to calm down. Now consider this finding when expecting players, coaches, and other participants to regain control (under competition terms and conditions)!*

EXAMPLE: *Sometimes, with only one gesture, look, or word you can induce and stimulate a self-regulatory attempt from players. If you notice self-regulatory attempts from players (and coaches), take this into consideration and appreciation. If a player self-regulates himself or herself quickly, you do not need to sanction them for a gesture or reaction, because they have already complied with your decision. This is a great part of 'game control' – being capable and mature to understand what is behind emotions, emotional reactions and their regulation in a competitive environment!*

**Reflective questions:**

Do you take into consideration self-regulatory attempts from players and coaches when you recognize them?

Do you usually restrain yourself from giving a sanction before it is necessary or do you have a fast trigger when doing so?

*"We may be unable to control our emotions, but we may be able to make changes to the things that trigger them and the behavior they lead to."*
(Paul Ekman)

According to Deckers (2018), **emotional regulation** is a specific type of coping that refers to control of our emotions in the following ways:

- Which emotions to experience?
- When to express them?
- How intensely?
- In which way?

These are important pieces of information for referees, especially in competitive environments where participants have to cope with different stressful situations in order to perform well, to be better than the opponent, to win the game.

Players and coaches (and other participants) should also be aware and understand in which way and how intensively are they allowed (according to the rules) to express their emotions.

"Which?" and "When?" will for sure happen, but "How intensively?" and in "In which way?" are important to understand for the application of the rules, and therefore 'control of the game'.

# EMOTIONAL INTELLIGENCE

According to authors Mayer and Salovey (1997), emotional intelligence involves four sets of abilities:

1) The ability to perceive accurately, appraise, and express emotion
2) The ability to access and/or generate feelings to facilitate thinking
3) The ability to understand emotions and emotional knowledge
4) The ability to regulate emotions to promote emotional and intellectual growth

In addition, emotional intelligence is the ability to **identify** how people feel, to **use** emotions to help you think, to **understand** the causes of emotions, and to include and **manage** emotions in your decision making the optimal choices in life (Salovey and Caruso, 2004).

Daniel Coleman (2000) describes emotional intelligence as the ability to manage ourselves and our relationships effectively. It consists of four fundamental capabilities:

**SELF-AWARENESS**: the ability to read and understand your emotions, to evaluate your strengths and limitations, and have a strong and positive sense of self-worth.

**SELF-MANAGEMENT**: the ability to have self-control of disruptive emotions and impulses, to display honesty and integrity, to manage yourself and your responsibilities, to adjust to changing situations and overcoming obstacles, to meet internal standards of excellence, to seize opportunities.

**SOCIAL AWARENESS:** the ability to have empathy and to recognize other people's perspective and needs.

**SOCIAL SKILL:** the ability to communicate effectively and resolve possible conflicts, to collaborate with others and build relationships.

Empathy is described as sensing other people's emotions, understanding their perspective, and taking active interest in their concerns (Goleman, 2000), as well as appreciating the difference in how people feel about things (Goleman, 2009).

To become aware, to perceive, and to understand emotions in self and in others is an important part of game control and self-regulation during the game. It is our responsibility to learn these skills and to become emotionally intelligent – for the sake of the game.

# Chapter 4

## BEHAVIOR

**How can behavior be predicted? What kinds of consequences, when experienced, increase or decrease the frequency of a certain behavior?**

Behavior is usually defined as a response to external or internal stimuli. Behavior can be visible – we can easily see and observe what another person is doing – or invisible – private, internal activities that cannot be readily observed by others, such as feeling and thinking while doing something (Martin and Pear, 2015; Ramnero and Torneke, 2008).

The dynamic interaction between a person and a situation is considered to be the best predictor of behavior. When describing behavior, there is always "Where?" and "When?", "How often?" and "How much?" In order to gain an understanding of the function of behaviors, we need to know "How?" behaviors 'move'. When do specific behaviors increase or decrease in frequency?

When observing behavior, it is important to notice:

- What happened?
- When and where?
- What did the person do?
- How often and how much?
- What happened afterward?

It is also important to mention the **quality** vs **quantity** of behavior. Quality refers to how well the person does it, while quantity refers to how much a person does something. Intrinsic motivation increases the quality of behavior more (how well a person does it), while extrinsic motivation increases the quantity (how much a person does something) (Deckers, 2018).

# ABC OF HUMAN BEHAVIOR

The ABCs of human behavior are very well described by authors Ramnero and Torneke (2008):

**A stands for ANTECEDENT**, that is, an event that occurs prior to a behavior: *When or in what situation does the person do it? In the presence or absence of what does the person do it?*

**B stands for BEHAVIOR**: *What is the person doing?*

**C stands for CONSEQUENCE** that follows the behavior: *What happens after the person does it*? Or: *What events follow upon doing it?*

These questions are vital. If we are to explain behavior, we must detect its function. *What purpose does the behavior serve?*

Behavior is usually governed by consequences of earlier, similar behavior, and depends on the situation. In the presence of A, B leads to C. If we detect a purpose or a function of a certain behavior, and the context in which it appears, we will understand it better.

**Reflective questions:**

What consequences result from our interaction with players, coaches, participants?

How do those consequences affect specific behaviors and under what circumstances?

*"When anger rises, think of the consequences."*
(Confucius)

We are in constant contact with the consequences of our own behavior. Consequences affect behavior in many ways. They can increase or decrease the likelihood of certain behavior, and consequences to certain behavior can be added or removed.

Before going further with explanations about behavior and consequences, I would like to introduce you to a few very influential behaviorism theories: *the law of effect, classical conditioning, and operant conditioning.*

# THE LAW OF EFFECT

The law of effect, proposed by psychologist Edward Thorndike in 1898, suggested that:

a) Behaviors that are immediately followed by pleasant and favorable consequences are more likely to occur again, for instance *being praised by a teacher for doing your homework will make you more likely to do your homework again.*

b) Behaviors that are followed by unpleasant and unfavorable consequences are less likely to occur again, for instance *if a person does not pay a parking fee and afterwards receives a ticket, they are less likely to repeat the same behavior – not paying for parking – in the future.*

Thorndike's discovery had a major influence on the development of behaviorism and better understanding of human behavior.

# CLASSICAL CONDITIONING

The term 'classical conditioning' refers to a learning process that occurs through associations between an environmental stimulus and natural involuntary response. This process is not under our control because involuntary automatic response or behavior is automatically triggered by a stimulus.

Classical conditioning was studied by Russian physiologist Ivan Pavlov (1897) during his research on the digestion of dogs. Pavlov found that when natural, unconditioned, involuntary stimulus (US), e.g. food, is presented to a dog, he starts to salivate, which is a natural, involuntary, unconditioned response (UR), and not learned behavior. If a neutral stimulus (NS), e.g. the sound of a bell, is presented to the dog, there is no response. If bell ringing (NS) is presented together with food (US), the dog shows the unconditioned, natural response (UR) of salivation. If bell ringing is presented once more, even without food, the dog starts to salivate because it associates bell ringing with food. Now bell ringing becomes a conditioned stimulus (CS) that produces the conditioned response (CR) of salivation. Dogs learned to expect food at the sound of the bell. Under normal conditions, the sight and smell of food causes a dog to salivate, and food is an unconditioned stimulus, while salivation is an unconditioned response. However, when we pair an unconditional stimulus like food with something that was previously neutral, like the sound of a bell, that neutral stimulus becomes a conditioned stimulus. Pavlov noticed that learning occurred faster when the interval between the CS (the sound of a bell) and the appearance of the US (food) was shorter.

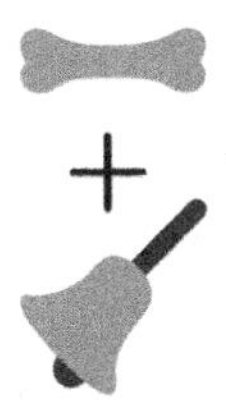

*Figure 7.* Classical conditioning

EXAMPLE: *You went to a sea food restaurant last week. You had some shellfish and ended up vomiting and becoming extremely ill and discovered you are allergic to shellfish. Now, whenever you drive by a sea food restaurant, you start to feel sick.*

EXAMPLE: *You were at a party and met a really nice person. While a certain song was playing, the two of you were dancing and instantly fell in love. Now, whenever you hear that specific song, you feel loving and think about your partner.*

EXAMPLE: *You like going to your grandmother's because she makes you feel happy. Last time when you were with your grandmother, the two of you baked a chocolate cake and had a really great time. Now, whenever you taste chocolate cake, you remember your grandmother and feel happy.*

# OPERANT CONDITIONING

Burrhus Frederic Skinner believed that classical conditioning was too simplistic to describe and explain the complexity of human behavior and proposed an approach called operant conditioning (1938). Operant conditioning is a type of learning where the consequences of your behavior shape your future behavior.

Skinner was influenced by Thorndike's law of effect, and believed that the best way to understand behavior was to look at the causes of an action and its consequences. Those consequences are either reinforcers or punishments, and he suggested that behavior can be modified when certain behavior is rewarded or sanctioned.

In operant conditioning, behaviors that are reinforced are strengthened and are more likely to occur in the future, while those that are punished are weakened and are less likely to occur in the future.

This leaves us with four basic ways to affect behavior (Skinner, 1953):

- **POSITIVE REINFORCEMENT**: The addition (or increase) of a certain consequence increases the likelihood of a certain behavior.
- **NEGATIVE REINFORCEMENT**: The removal (or decrease) of a certain consequence increases the likelihood of a certain behavior.
- **POSITIVE PUNISHMENT**: The addition (or increase) of a certain consequence decreases the likelihood of a certain behavior.
- **NEGATIVE PUNISHMENT**: The removal (or decrease) of a certain consequence decreases the likelihood of a certain behavior.

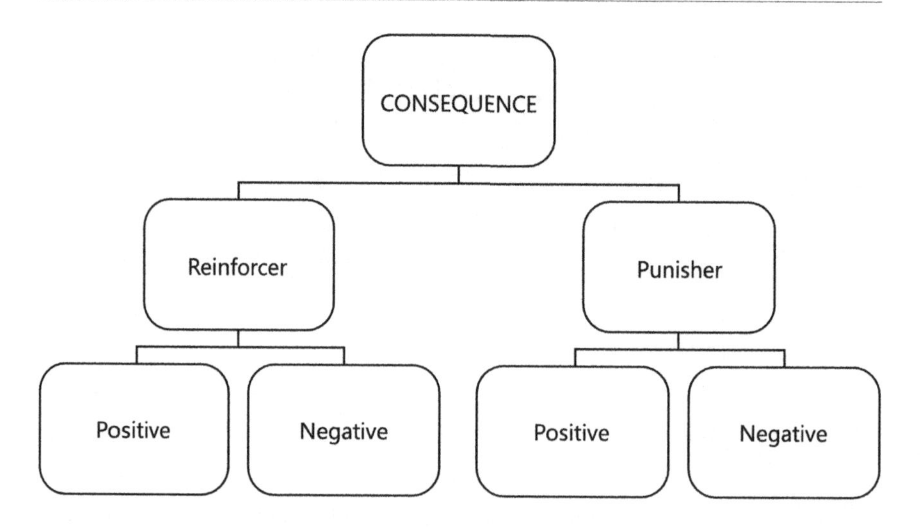


*Figure 8.* Consequences as reinforcers and punishers

## REINFORCERS

They increase the probability for a desired behavior to occur again. They occur after the behavior and increase the chance that the behavior will be repeated.

Reinforcers add (positive) or remove something (negative) to strengthen the response and desired behavior.

> Positive and negative reinforcement cannot be equated with the adjectives "positive" and "negative" in an evaluative sense.

Positive and negative reinforcement cannot be equated with the adjectives "positive" and "negative" in an evaluative sense, where "positive" means good and "negative" means bad. This is probably the most common misunderstanding of positive and negative reinforcement. When using these terms, it is important to remember that "positive" means the addition (or increase) of a certain consequence that has a reinforcing or punishing effect on behavior when applied. "Negative" means that the removal (or decrease) of a certain consequence that has a reinforcing or punishing effect on behavior (Martin and Pear, 2015).

**Positive reinforcers** are favorable events or outcomes for an individual following desired behavior. They strengthen behavior by providing a consequence the individual finds rewarding.

<u>EXAMPLE:</u> *When a player receives praise from the coach in front of the whole team after playing defense successfully, he or she is more likely to put in extra effort when playing defense again in another game.*

<u>EXAMPLE:</u> *If you do an excellent job at work, your boss gives you a bonus on your paycheck, and you will more likely continue with your good work.*

**Negative reinforcers** are characterized by the removal of an undesired or unpleasant outcome after desired behavior. The response is strengthened as something considered negative is removed. They reinforce behavior because they remove an unpleasant experience.

EXAMPLE: *When you do not use your seat belt, you receive a fine of 50 €. To avoid paying a fine, you fasten your seat belt every time when you drive.*

EXAMPLE: *A student is using a mobile phone during the lecture. The professor takes their phone and the student's misbehavior will decrease. To avoid getting their phone taken away from them again, the student puts the phone in a bag and focuses on the lecture.*

We have two basic functional relationships (the relation between behavior and reinforcer) (Ramnero and Torneke, 2008):

- **Avoidance**, when the function of a certain behavior is to avoid confronting an aversive stimulus.

- **Escape**, when the function of a certain behavior is to get away from or in some other way lessen the influence of a present aversive stimulus. Escape and avoidance behaviors function on negative reinforcement.

Money is a generalized reinforcer, because we associate money with access to other stimuli. Money has great potential for influencing human behavior.

For maximum effectiveness, a reinforcer should be given immediately after the desired response. Delayed reinforcers may have an effect on behavior because of instructions about the behavior leading to the reinforcer, and/or because of self-statements (or "thoughts") that intervene between that behavior and the delayed reinforcer (Martin and Pear, 2015).

<u>EXAMPLE:</u> *When you are officiating at a tournament, World Cup for instance, you should establish the professional criteria for measures like a technical foul, 2 min, or red card the first game on the first day of the tournament. It will help players and coaches to faster adopt and modify behavior to avoid being sanctioned. If you and your colleague referees set the criteria for the rest of the tournament, the players and coaches will know what is allowed and what is not. If you keep those criteria (the same criteria) every day during the tournament, it will be more likely that they will obey them, and less likely that misbehavior will occur. Or at least less frequently.*

The likelihood of emitting a behavior that has been reinforced under given circumstances increases also in situations similar to the original one. We call this generalization (Ramnero and Torneke, 2008).

In the presence of A (also *A*, **A,** a, and @) B leads to C

*Figure 9.* Generalization (Source: The ABC's of human behavior, Ramnero and Torneke, 2008)

The opposite of generalization is discriminatory learning (Ramnero and Torneke, 2008). Most behaviors are only followed by reinforcement under certain circumstances.

In the presence of A (but not *A*, **A,** a, and @) B leads to C

*Figure 10.* Discriminatory learning (Source: The ABC's of Human Behavior, Ramnero and Torneke, 2008)

The central questions are always these: What is the function of behavior (B)? When was this? Was there anything else earlier that you think may have had an effect on events?

There are also **secondary reinforcers** – something that strengthens a behavior because it leads to a primary reinforcer (Martin and Pear, 2015). For instance, a token economy system is a system in which targeted behaviors are reinforced with tokens, e.g. *stickers, points, coupons* (secondary reinforcer) and later exchanged for rewards, e.g. *discounts, money, rewards* (primary reinforcers).

<u>EXAMPLE:</u> *A child has a deal with their parents to receive a 'star sticker' after every completed homework. When the child collects 20 stickers, the parents will buy them a favorite toy. To get the favorite toy, the child starts to complete homework regularly.*

**Reflective questions:**

Imagine if there was a rule that teams/clubs collect extra points for showing desirable behavior on and off the court. Teams with fewer red cards, 2-minute suspensions, or fouls would be rewarded with extra money or top sponsor for their behavior.

What do you think, would this decrease the likelihood of that unsportsmanlike behavior during games?

Would they start to play more fairly in the future? Or would there be no significant changes in their behavior during games?

## PUNISHERS

They decrease the probability of an undesired behavior to occur again, or they extinguish the behavior. Punishers add (positive) or remove something (negative) that will stop a response from happening again or weaken the response and undesired behavior.

Punishment is when the increase of something undesirable attempts to cause a decrease in the behavior that follows. It weakens or eliminates certain behavior. Like reinforcers, punishment can work either by applying an unpleasant stimulus (positive punisher) or by removing a potentially rewarding stimulus (negative punisher). In punishment, 'positive' means adding something, 'negative' means taking something away.

**Positive punishment** is when unfavorable events or outcomes are given in order to weaken the response that follows. It implies adding an unpleasant consequence to decrease a behavior.

EXAMPLE: *A player is late to practice and the coach orders her to do 50 push-ups. The player is less likely to be late to practice next time because she does not want to do extra push-ups.*

EXAMPLE: *A coach would receive fines last season every time a technical foul was called against him. This season, no technical fouls have been called against him. His misbehavior decreased after paying fines.*

**Negative punishment** is characterized by the removal of a favorable event or outcome after an undesired behavior occurs. It implies removing or taking away a pleasant consequence. Punishers weaken your response or decrease your behavior.

EXAMPLE: *You lose your driving license if an alcohol test shows you had unpermitted amounts of alcohol in your blood while driving a car. This consequence should decrease your behavior of driving after a few glasses of alcohol.*

<u>EXAMPLE:</u> *A child's favorite toy or video game is taken away after they show misbehavior. In the future, the child will be less likely to misbehave in order to keep their toy or video game.*

Note that the technical meaning of the word 'punishment' for behavior modifiers is quite specific and differs in three ways from the common meaning of the word for most people (Martin and Pear, 2015):

- It occurs immediately after the problem behavior.
- It is not a form of moral sanction, vengeance, retribution.
- It is not used to deter others from engaging in the target behavior.

Martin and Pear (2015) proposed certain ways to deliver the punishers:

1) The punisher should be presented immediately following the undesirable behavior.
2) The punisher should be presented following every instance of the undesirable behavior.
3) The delivery of the punisher should not be paired with positive reinforcement.
4) The person administering the punisher should remain calm when doing so.

The last, fourth principle is highly important for referees to keep in mind, because a calm and professional approach when presenting a punisher – a 'sanction' (e.g. *red card, 2 min suspension, TF, or UF*) makes clear to the recipient that the punishment is not being administered out of anger or for other irrelevant reasons, but because of inappropriate behavior with respect to the rules.

<u>EXAMPLE</u>: *If a referee presenting a 'punisher' – a sanction for unsportsman-like behavior – and shows anger and frustration, he or she may reinforce the undesirable behavior or inappropriately change this consequence. The players and coaches could become even more frustrated, expressing anger and discontent, which may result in even worse consequences. A calm, professional approach helps ensure that a punishment is presented appropriately.*

Sometimes punishers do not necessarily lead toward desired behavior, because they only tell you what not to do, while reinforcers tell you what to do. They can create potentially harmful side effects, such as fear, avoidance, or escape, or increase aggression (as a way to cope with the consequence). A punished behavior is usually not forgotten, but it is suppressed – if the punishment is no longer present, the behavior returns.

*"A person who has been punished is not thereby simply less inclined to behave in a given way; at best, he learns how to avoid punishment."*
(B. F. Skinner)

## DIFFERENCE BETWEEN CLASSICAL AND OPERANT CONDITIONING

Operant behavior is voluntary, controlled by the consequence, while classical conditioning involves involuntary response automatically triggered by a stimulus (not under control).

Classical conditioning is learning by association, while operant conditioning is learning by consequence.

In classical conditioning, behaviors are modified through the association of stimuli (association between a particular response and a stimuli), whereas in operant conditioning, behaviors are modified by reward or punishment (association between a particular behavior and a consequence).

# LEARNING BEHAVIOR THROUGH MODELING

A large amount of learning occurs through observation, imitation, and interactions with other people. The social learning theory presented by Albert Bandura (1977) suggests that much of human behavior is learned through modeling, rather than only through reinforcement, rewards, or punishment. People can learn automatically through observation, and learning is achieved by mentally rehearsing and then imitating the observed actions of other people, who serve as models of appropriate or acceptable behavior.

According to Bandura, children learn how to behave while imitating the behavior of others. Children are highly likely to receive positive reinforcement for the type of behavior that is considered most appropriate to their culture and their gender.

Bandura believed that children learn aggression through observing and imitating the violent acts of adults, particularly family members.

There are four processes we need to take in consideration while speaking about learning through observation (Bandura and Jeffrey, 1973):

- **ATTENTION** – learning requires that the learner is paying attention to the behavior in the first place
- **RETENTION** – the ability to store information and to remember what he/she saw or heard
- **MOTOR REPRODUCTION** – to actually able to perform and physically reproduce the observed behavior
- **MOTIVATION** – to have a good motive to reproduce it (external and internal reinforcements)

Actions of others can influence our behavior, especially in social settings and specific contexts (we applaud when others clap, we laugh when others laugh) (Bandura, 1977).

People differ in the degree to which their behavior is guided by modeling influences, and not all models are equally effective and influential. We are more likely to imitate models who (Bandura, 1977):

- We admire and respect
- Have authority and power positions, with high social status
- Have competence and are rewarded for their behavior (performance)
- Are similar to us in age, gender, and interests

People who lack confidence and self-esteem, who are dependent, and who have been frequently rewarded for imitativeness are more likely to adopt the behavior of successful models. Perceptive and confident people readily imitate both idealized models and those whose behavior is highly useful. When modeling is used to develop competencies, the more talented, daring, and adventurous individuals will have greater benefits from observation of models (Bandura, 1977).

Exposure to the behavior of appropriate models is one of the most effective ways to enhance the acquisition of new behavior patterns and skills (Mischel, 1996).

<u>EXAMPLE:</u> *Young players like to imitate their role models in how they dress, behave, and communicate on and off the court. Children and teenagers observe what 'important others' (parents, coaches, teachers, role models, peers, etc.) are doing and they tend to repeat observed behavior. This is really important when talking about aggressive behavior. The more they observe aggressive behavior in 'important others', the more likely it is that they will do it themselves.*

Although undesirable behavior, such as aggression and violence, can be learned through observing and imitating others, in many ways we can encourage positive, desirable behavior to be learned and adopted. By observing the consequences produced by the behavior patterns of others, the observer learns about the outcomes that would probably happen if they produced similar behaviors themselves (Mischel, 1996).

Observing others do something inappropriate may teach us demonstrate that kind of behavior. It can teach us what not to do.

EXAMPLE: *Three kids on the playground watch how another kid gets reprimanded for hitting another child. They learn from observing this situation that they should not hit others.*

## HOW CAN BEHAVIOR BE PREDICTED?

Does personality predict behavior or does behavior reveal personality?

Walter Mischel (1968) proposed that analysis of a person's behavior, in different situations, observed on numerous occasions, would provide clues to behavior patterns that would reveal a distinctive signature of personality. **The dynamic interaction between a person and the situation** is the best predictor of behavior.

Personality is just one of many factors that guide our behavior. Looking at personality traits alone gives us a few clues, but there are also many external factors, such as context, that we need to take in consideration (Collin et al., 2012). Culture, upbringing, environment, our experiences, and our motivation also influence our actions. Different contexts and different situations produce different behavior. Behavior is always affected by the context in which it is evoked.

Behaviors depend on highly specific events but remain stable when the consequences to which they lead remain similar. If the conditions do not change drastically and if there is a stability in personality, **past behavior tends to be the best predictor of future behavior in similar situations** (Mischel, 1996).

<u>EXAMPLE:</u> *A certain coach usually shows more misbehavior and receives more sanctions during play-off games than during regular season. Their team was eliminated past 3 seasons after the play-off games and never had a chance to win the championship, which made the coach very frustrated. If the coach does not change the way they deal with the pressure of the play-offs, and self-regulate frustration, they will probably behave the same as usual during the end of the season (when everything is at stake).*

EXAMPLE: *A referee gets upset when they receive a nomination to officiate with a certain colleague or a certain team. If the referee does not try to change their interpretation of that event or does not gain a new (better) experience officiating with that colleague or team, their behavior will be similar every time upon receiving that nomination – they will get upset. If the referee changes their 'point of view' – the perception of that event – or has a better experience in the last game (with that colleague or team), the behavior will be likely to change.*

**Reflective questions:**

When preparing to officiate a certain game or match, do you usually prepare yourself for the characteristics of the participants you are going to officiate?

Do you prepare how to manage an 'aggressive coach', 'emotional player', or 'inexperienced colleague'?

Think about how your preparation for certain behavior can help you officiate better and keep the game (match) under control.

*"It is possible to change your behavior through changing your thinking, and to change your thinking by changing your behavior."*
(Albert Ellis)

When it comes to predicting behavior and expecting someone to behave in certain ways, it is important not to overuse your preparation in a way to take some actions before a certain behavior occurs.

EXAMPLE: *If you prepare yourself to expect a certain behavior from a specific coach, you should be aware not to react and jump to conclusions even before that behavior occurs. Sometimes, expecting a (mis)behavior to happen, for example a complaint from a coach, you can act in ways that make the expected behavior more likely to occur, like ignoring the coach or being arrogant in the communication with them.*

In many cases of 'predicting' our behavior or that of others, we need to be aware of self-fulfilling prophecy. Self-fulfilling prophecy is a belief that comes true because we are acting like it is already true creating the consequence that is based on our previous experience. It is a prediction that causes itself to be true due to the belief, expectations and the behavior of the believer.

EXAMPLE: *If you start doubting your ability to officiate a game, you may subconsciously sabotage yourself by not preparing enough. You can avoid preparing for that game since you believe that the game will be doomed anyway. Therefore, you probably will not officiate successfully.*

*"It is our attitude at the beginning of the task which more than anything will affect a successful outcome."*
(William James)

Cultural norms can also shape our behavior. Social rules and sanctions are usually deliberately formal and constant. They facilitate consistencies in social behavior. Social institutions, like schools, military service, and prisons, tend to have fixed-rule systems according to which outcomes are dispensed fairly and constantly at different times for similar behaviors (Mischel, 1996). Even in sports, we can find fixed-rule systems. Teams, clubs, and leagues tend to have their own rule systems that they apply during competitions.

EXAMPLE: *A certain handball team has a rule regarding being late to the practice. Every time when any player of that team arrives late to the practice, they face the same consequences, for example doing extra sprints.*

EXAMPLE: *A certain basketball league has a rule that any technical foul committed by any participant would be sanctioned additionally with a fine, for instance paying 500 $ after the game in which the technical foul was committed.*

# SELF-REGULATING BEHAVIOR

Self-regulation can be defined as an ability to regulate our thoughts, emotions, and behaviors to help us attain our personal goals (Zimmerman, 2000).

Learning how to self-regulate is a skill that we learn during our life through our upbringing, education, experience, and social connections. It is also related to our values, the culture we live in, and the occupational demands of a job we do.

The ability to manage dysfunctional reactions and behavior for the purpose of acting more appropriately and maturely can be crucial in many situations. The ability to think before acting and make a plan before taking an action is really important also for the referees.

EXAMPLE: *In a situation of conflict between two players, many emotions arise together with inappropriate behaviors. It is important for the referee to stay calm and regulate own reactions and behavior, and to take proper actions that will resolve (and sanction) the conflict in a professional and appropriate way (according to the rules of the sport).*

According to Daniel Goleman (1998), self-regulation refers to handling and managing impulses and dealing with distressing feelings. These skills are at the core of five emotional competencies:

- **Self-control** – managing disruptive emotions and impulses effectively
- **Trustworthiness** – displaying honesty and integrity
- **Conscientiousness** – dependability and responsibility in fulfilling obligations
- **Adaptability** – flexibility in handling change and challenges
- **Innovation** – being open to novel ideas, approaches, and new information

Self-regulatory processes are also often learned through a social learning process in which a novice (less expert person) observes and imitates the self-regulatory skills of an expert model (Reeve, 2009). Observing an experienced, role-model referee can help you to try to implement similar actions in a self-regulatory process during your officiating performance. It does not mean that you need to copy the other referee's behavior but to try to implement successful methods into your own officiating style.

*"Smart people learn from everything and everyone, average people from their experience, stupid people already have all the answers."*
(Socrates)

# Chapter 5

## PERSONALITY

**Who am I? How do people differ from each other? What are the personality types? How do we express them?**

Personality is one of the most important assets we have, helping us shape our past experiences and influencing future ones. All our achievements in the past and expectations we have for the future can be influenced by our personality and the characteristics of the other people we interact with. If we want to better understand human nature and behavior, it is essential to also understand personality.

Psychologist Lawrence A. Pervin (2003) defined personality as a complex organization of cognitions, affects, and behaviors that gives direction and patterns to a person's life. It consists of both structures and processes, reflects both nature (genes) and nurture (experience), and includes the effects of the past, as well as the constructions of the present and the future.

According to Mischel, Shoda, and Ayduk (2008), personality construct includes the following aspects:

- Personality shows continuity, stability, and coherence.

- Personality is expressed in many ways – from behavior through thoughts and feelings.
- Personality is a determinant that influences how the individual relates to the social world.
- Personality is a psychological concept, but it is also assumed to link with the physical, biological characteristics of the person.

There are many definitions of the term, but investigators generally agree that personality is a dynamic and organized set of characteristics possessed by a person that uniquely influences his or her cognitions, motivations, and behaviors in various situations (Ryckman, 2008).

When describing personality, it is important to mention the term '**personality dynamics**'. Personality dynamics include individuals' adaptation or adjustment to the demands of life and have major implications for psychological health. Modern personality theory considers cognitive processes as a major aspect of personality dynamics. How we think is an important determinant of our choices and adaptation (Cloninger, 2004).

*Adaptation – an individual's way of coping with the world, of adjusting to demands and opportunities in the environment.*

The multiple influences on the personality system include the interactive effects of biological determinants, learning, and social and cultural influences (Mischel et al., 2008). The results of heritability studies suggest that there are fairly strong genetic influences on personality characteristics (Ashton, 2018).

Therefore, both '**nature and nurture**' have an important role in personal development and growth. Our inherited biological blueprint and the environment we live in have an impact on our personality and behavior.

**Reflective questions:**

In your opinion, does nature or nurture have more impact on someone's personality? What do you see in yourself?

Did your upbringing and culture shaped your personality more, or did you inherit most of who you are?

It is important to mention that environmental influences on personality include not only family experience and the way a child is raised but also a variety of other influences received from outside of family, through experiences in the environment that surrounds us (Ashton, 2018).

The characteristics of the culture we live in are also important for our adaptation to environment. Culture influences us through its opportunities and expectations (Cloninger, 2004), by affecting the ways in which we react to individuals' behavior (Mischel, et al., 2008). The ways people interpret situations and how they respond to those experiences can largely depend on the characteristics of the culture they live in.

*"Everything that irritates us about others*
*can lead us to an understanding of ourselves."*
(Carl Jung)

In the course of history, a variety of approaches and different perspectives on studying personality and its development have emerged. Together they provide distinctive insights to the understanding of human nature and the person "as a whole". Here are their descriptions (Cloninger, 2004; Mischel, et al., 2008):

**THE BIOLOGICAL PERSPECTIVE** tries to specify the role of genetic determinants and answer the question "How much of personality reflects nature, inheritance, and biological predispositions?" and of the social environment in a way to understand "To what extent is personality a reflection of nurture and life experiences?"

It reveals the importance of individuals' biological heritage. It opens the way to studying mind-brain-behavior links and their connections to individual differences in personality. What people think, feel, and do depends on their genes, neural connections, biochemistry – all in continuous interactions with the environment. At the same time, what people think, feel, and do changes their neural networks, biochemistry, and brain structure.

**THE PSYCHOANALYTICAL PERSPECTIVE** seeks to understand how unconscious motivations can influence our personality, behavior, and experience. It tries to answer the questions: "What are the real motives that drive our behavior?", "How can we explain irrational fears and anxieties?", "How much of what we do is without awareness?" It assumes that personality is strongly influenced by our unconscious determinants which originate from our early experiences, and that childhood experiences are important in determining personality.

**THE TRAIT PERSPECTIVE** focuses on one of the most fundamental questions: "How shall we describe people?", "Who am I like as a person?", "How am I different from other people?", "How does my personality influence the situations I choose to be in?" It seeks to identify the types of stable psychological qualities and behavioral dispositions that characterize different individuals and types consistently, that are more or less stable across time and across situations.

**Personality traits** *are continuous quantitative variables of a characteristic that varies from one person to another. A trait refers to a person's (more or less consistent) behavior across time and across relevant situations.*

**Personality types** *are categories or qualitative groupings of people with similar characteristics. Theoretically, a small number of types describe everyone.*

According to Deckers (2018), personality traits help answer two important questions:

1) Why do people react differently to the same situation?
2) Why do people differ in the situations they approach and avoid?

**THE BEHAVIORAL PERSPECTIVE** tries to analyze how external conditions and rewards influence and shape personality and behavior through learning process. It focuses on questions such as: "How my behavior and feelings can be modified with new learning experiences?", "How are behavior patterns, including emotions and fears learned?" The behavioral perspective assumes that behavior is readily influenced by specific situations and by the consequences or reinforcers to which behavior leads. Changing those consequences in turn modifies behavior in predictable ways. Personality is defined in terms of behavior – what a person does constitutes his or her personality.

**THE COGNITIVE PERSPECTIVE** assumes that people differ from one another in how they think about themselves and the people around them and that those cognitions are key variables in understanding personality differences. The specific focus is on the individual's characteristic ways of thinking and processing information, both cognitively and emotionally: "How does what I know, think, and feel about myself and the social world influence what I do and can become?", "What can I do to change how I think and feel?", "How can I enhance my control over my life?" The mental processes such as thinking, knowledge, and memory are important for personality development.

**THE COGNITIVE SOCIAL LEARNING PERSPECTIVE** expands on themes of importance of language and social environment, and how social knowledge is used in dealing with the world, in the construction of the self, in self-regulation, and self-control. Personality is formed through interaction with the environment, and behavior is environmentally determined and situation-specific.

**THE HUMANISTIC PERSPECTIVE** in personality theory values the subjective experience of the individual, including emotional experience. It focuses on "higher", more developed, and healthier aspects of human experience and their development, among which are spirituality, creativity, and tolerance. It requires studying the internal or mental processes through which individuals interpret experience: "Who am I really? How do I see myself? How do I see my parents", "Am I happy and fulfilled? Where am I going? Who do I want to become?"

In sum, the humanistic approach tends to view "healthy people" as those who (Mischel, et al. 2008):

- Become aware of themselves, their feelings, and their limits; accept themselves, their lives, and what they make of their lives as their own responsibility
- Have "the courage to be"
- Experience the "here and now"; are not trapped to live in the past or to dwell in the future through anxious expectations and distorted defenses

Considering all this, there are many theories of personality. Here are presented some influential ones:

# ID, EGO, SUPEREGO

The 'father of psychoanalysis', Sigmund Freud, believed that our personality is shaped by early childhood experiences that are consciously and unconsciously processed through developmental stages. In his work *The Ego and the Id* (1923), he presented his structural model of the psyche. Our psyche, according to Freud, resembles an iceberg (*Figure 11.*), structured with three parts – id, ego, and superego – that form the psychodynamic structure of personality. Under the surface, a person's personality represents the deeply internal struggles and constant conflict between id, ego, and superego.

**ID** – hidden in the unconscious, controls our drives and impulses, and represents an urge that demands instant satisfaction. A large part of our personality consists of unconscious desires that we want to satisfy. Freud considered the id to be the original aspect of our personality.

**EGO** – negotiates with the id and pleases the superego. The ego's main function is to mediate between the id's demands and the reality which says we can't have everything we desire but must take into account the world we live in. It is located in all three areas of our mind – the conscious, preconscious and unconscious.

**SUPEREGO** – represents the internalized moral standards, values, and ideals of society as conveyed by the parents. The superego controls the ego and is a judging force, the source of our conscience, guilt, and shame. The main functions of the superego are to inhibit the urges of the id, to persuade the ego to substitute moralistic goals for realistic ones, and to strive for perfection. According to Freud, a person's conscience comes from their parents or a parental figure (important others). As the person grows, they internalize their standards and moral codes.

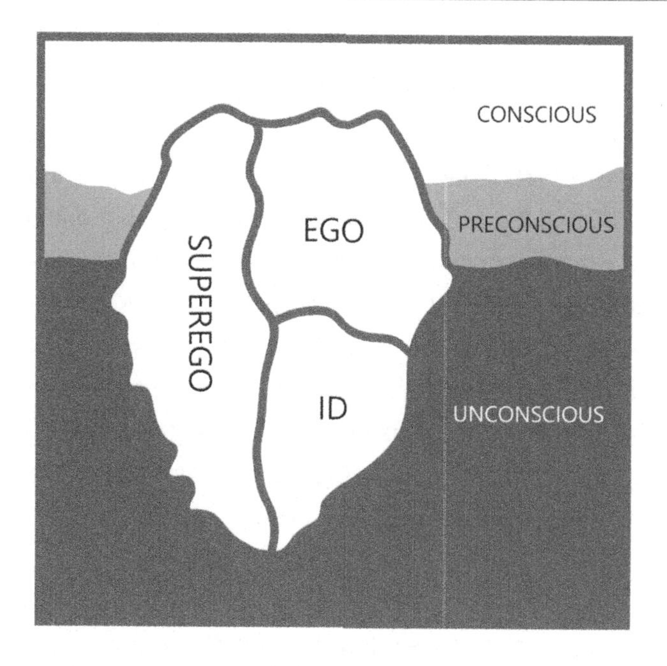


*Figure 11.* Structural model of the psyche

*"The only person with whom you have to compare yourself*
*is you in the past. One day, in retrospective,*
*the years of struggle will strike you*
*as the most beautiful."*
(Sigmund Freud)

Freud also believed that two basic drives have direct control over our minds and shape our personality:

- **Love (Eros)** - 'Eros' represents love and the instinct to survive
- **Aggression (Thanatos)** - 'Thanatos' represents aggression, which instinctively leads to death

# EGO DEFENSE MECHANISMS

Anna Freud developed the concept of 'ego defense mechanisms' (1937). She described the mechanisms people use to psychologically defend themselves against anxiety provoked by conflicts of everyday life. How we cope with anxiety, how we protect ourselves from painful thoughts, impulses, or urges are the issues that represent the basics of personality. If our ego cannot deal with the demands of our desires and moral standards, we feel anxious. We develop strategies to distort reality and exclude feelings from awareness so that we do not feel anxious anymore. She proposed several important defense mechanisms, which we use unconsciously most of the time. When we use them, they represent our psychological defense for our ego's survival.

- **Denial** – involves denying the existence of an external threat or traumatic event. Unpleasant reality is ignored. For instance, *we may be in denial and refuse to acknowledge that a loved one has died. We can live in this denial for days, months, or even longer.*

- **Displacement** – involves shifting unconscious impulses and frustration from threatening objects or people to objects or people that are less threatening, like *replacing hostility toward one's boss with hostility towards one's partner.*

- **Projection** – involves attributing a disturbing urge or unacceptable desire to someone else. For example, *if you are mad at someone, you may accuse that person of being mad at you.*

- **Rationalization** – involves justifying our unacceptable behavior or disturbing thought or feeling to make it more logical, acceptable, and less threatening to us. For instance, *a young referee may learn that he or she was not nominated for the upcoming U17 World Championship* *because of poor officiating in the last few games, and comes to the conclusion that he or she did not really want to go there because it is 'just a U17 cup'.*

- **Reaction formation** – involves expressing an impulse that is opposite to true feelings or motives, such as *being nice to someone who you do not really like.*
- **Regression** – involves returning to an earlier, less frustrating period of life and displaying usually childish behaviors. For example, *a seven-year-old child may start to climb on his or her mother on the first day of school, or a forty-year old person with marital difficulties may move back to his or her parents and live with them.*
- **Repression** – involves unconscious denial of the existence of something that causes anxiety, like an emotionally difficult situation or unpleasant experience, for instance *a traumatic experience in childhood may never be remembered.*
- **Sublimation** – involves transforming or displacing unacceptable motives into constructive socially acceptable behaviors, for instance *a desire for expressing aggression transforms into taking self-defense lessons.*

**Reflective questions:**

Which of the defense mechanisms do you see in yourself?

Which of them you do recognize in your friends, partner, or coworkers?

Which ones have you recognized in a sports officiating environment?

# STAGES OF PSYCHOSOCIAL DEVELOPMENT

Psychologist Erik Erikson viewed personality as a product of individual's experiences, social interactions, and the choices a person makes in life. He proposed that human personality develops through eight distinct and predetermined stages between birth and death (1950, 1963). Each stage presents a challenge or a crisis in which people experience a conflict that serves as a turning point in development. In each stage, the choices you make have a strong impact on your development – you go either in one direction or another. Failure at any stage results in some deficiencies, such as lack of trust or sense of guilt, that stay with you throughout life. Overcoming obstacles in each stage successfully, we develop as healthy individuals with a strong sense of self – we know who we are.

*"The richest and fullest lives attempt to achieve an*
*inner balance between three realms:*
*work, love and play."*
(Erik Erikson)

The eight stages of psychosocial development presented by Erikson (1950, 1963, 1998) are:

1) **TRUST VS. MISTRUST** (0–18 months old): this stage covers the period of infancy, the first months of a child's life. During this stage, the basic experience of interacting with a stable, consistent, and trustworthy caregiver turns into a basic trust of the world. If the relationship with the primary caregiver (especially with the mother) is predictable, warmth and stable, the baby develops a sense of trust, which "forms the basis of the child's sense of identity". This includes trusting yourself and knowing that, when caregivers are not available, you can take care of yourself. Caregivers who are emotionally unavailable and inconsistent can awake feelings of mistrust, which can

result in a feeling of fear and a sense that the world is inconsistent and unpredictable.

2) **AUTONOMY VS. SHAME AND DOUBT** (1–3 years old): when the child is 13 to 36 months old (early childhood), it starts to take some actions on its own and make simple decisions. If parents or caregivers allow children to make choices and gain control, children develop a sense of autonomy. If parents are too controlling, constantly telling children what not do and criticizing their attempts to make simple actions or choices, children may develop a sense of shame and doubt in themselves, feeling inadequate in terms of their abilities. Shame and doubt occur when the child feels incompetent with respect to its ability to complete a task. During this stage, it is important to allow children to do basic tasks "all by themselves". Children who are successful in this stage will be more confident in their abilities.

3) **INITIATIVE VS. GUILT** (3–6 years old): During the preschool years, children start to socially interact with peers, planning and creating their own games and activities. If they are allowed to take these actions, they will develop confidence in their ability to take initiative. If the child is not allowed to make certain decisions and complete their own actions, the sense of guilt develops. The child may even develop a sense of frustration for not being able to achieve a goal and may show aggressive behaviors, such as throwing or hitting objects, or yelling.

4) **COMPETENCE VS. INFERIORITY** (6–12 years old): During the school years, friends, peers, and teachers begin to have an important role in the child's life as a major source of child's self-esteem. The child compares its self-worth to others, especially in the classroom environment. If they demonstrate the competencies and abilities valued by society, they begin to develop a sense of pride and competence. Encouraging the child increases the feelings of adequacy and competency with

respect to the ability to reach goals. Restrictions and disapproval from teachers or parents lead to doubt, questioning, developing a sense of inferiority and incompetency. Competency, the chief virtue in this stage, is developed when a healthy balance between the two extremes is reached.

5) **IDENTITY VS. CONFUSION** (12–18 years old): During adolescence, teenagers explore their independence and the views of themselves. "Who am I?" "How do I fit in?" "Where am I going in life?" are the questions teenagers usually ask themselves. To find out who they really are, they explore personal values, beliefs, and goals, experimenting with different roles, activities, and behaviors. Erikson called this stage the identity crisis. If a teen receives proper encouragement and reinforcement, through personal exploration he or she will develop a solid sense of self and a clearer identity. If, however, parents and other important figures push a teenager to conform to their views, making them unsure of their beliefs, the teen will face identity confusion. Sometimes teenagers get lost in the confusing search for a genuine identity and never really feel a true sense of self. Identity crisis is the result of identity confusion and can cause the adolescent to try out different life styles. During this stage, the teen is also looking towards the future in terms of employment, relationships, and family. The sense of personal identity is shaped by our experiences and interactions with others, through which we learn the roles that are important to fit into society. Success in this stage will lead to a sense of fidelity, which is characterized by the ability to commit to others and accept others even with differences.

6) **INTIMACY VS. ISOLATION** (18–40 years old): According to Erikson, the primary task of personality development during adulthood is to find and develop intimacy with other people. Making commitment to others and caring about the needs of others are important tasks in this stage. Dating, marriage, family, and friendships are important

during this stage. Successful completion of this stage can result in happy relationships, and a sense of commitment and intimacy. It also involves feelings of safety and love. Those who fear commitment and fail to form lasting relationships may feel isolated and alone.

7) **GENERATIVITY VS. STAGNATION** (40–65 years old): at some point, a person needs to be needed and to feel like they are guiding the next generation. The desire to leave a legacy, create positive changes that will benefit other people develops during middle adulthood. During this time, if a person is enjoying raising their children and participating in activities, that gives them a sense of purpose and contribution to society. They will feel useful and productive and that they have 'made their mark' on the world. If a person is not comfortable with the way their life is progressing, or regrets some missed opportunities, they will feel useless, unproductive, and stagnant.

8) **INTEGRITY VS. DESPAIR** (65+ years old): During this stage, people often reflect on things they have accomplished. They think about whether their life was well spent or wasted. If someone feels a sense of satisfaction with the way they lived their life, they feel integrity, a basic sense of wholeness or of being complete. If one feels guilt about the past or that they failed to accomplish important goals, despair is likely to follow. Wisdom is the result of successfully accomplishing this final developmental task.

As we can see, according to Erikson, if people successfully deal with the conflicts in each stage, they come out with psychological strengths. If they fail to deal with these conflicts successfully, they may not develop the skills needed for a strong sense of self and adequate development.

# THREE DIMENSIONS THEORY

Psychologist Hans J. Eysenck suggested that individual differences in traits have a biological and inherited basis.
He proposed a personality theory based on three dimensions (Eysenck, 1947, 1981, 1985), defined as combinations of traits or factors:

**E – EXTRAVERSION** versus **INTROVERSION**
This personality dimension ranges from one end with outgoing, active, sociable, and talkative people (extravert) to the other end with reserved, quiet, careful, and shy persons (introverts). Most people have in some way both extrovert and introvert characteristics and fall in the middle, rather than at the extremes of the dimensions. Whether a person is more extravert or introvert has values of great quality and significance for our society, which they present in different ways.

**N – NEUROTICISM** versus **EMOTIONAL STABILITY**
This dimension describes people who tend to be moody, touchy, anxious, nervous, and easily upset at one end (neuroticism), and at the other end are people who are characterized as calm, reliable, and stable.

**P – PSYCHOTICISM** versus **IMPULS CONTROL**
People who score high in psychoticism are aggressive, impulsive, ego-centric, antisocial, and unemphatic. They also tend to be very creative. On the other hand, people who score low on psychoticism are more empathetic, altruistic, open-minded, kind, and reasonable.

# THE BIG FIVE MODEL

The Big Five personality traits model, also known under the acronym OCEAN, focuses on describing personality through five broad dimensions (Costa and McCrae, 1985, 1992): *Openness, Conscientiousness, Extraversion, Agreeableness, and Neuroticism.*

Among the many psychology researchers who have studied the Big Five model, Paul Costa and Robert McCrae developed a self-reported questionnaire, NEO-PI-R (1992), to measure a person's standing on each factor by computing how much they agree that various statements describe them. The five dimensions are:

**OPENNES TO EXPERIENCE** (curious vs. conventional)
People who are open to experience are curious, creative, imaginative, original, liberal, and willing to try new things (more likely to engage in risky behavior). On the other hand, people with low openness dislike change, resist new ideas, are uncreative, conservative, conventional, with narrow interests.

**CONSCIENTIOUSNESS** (dependable vs. careless)
People with high conscientiousness are more likely to regulate their reactions showing more self-discipline and self-control. They are organized, on-time, dependable, and prepared. People with low conscientiousness are usually not reliable, dislike structure and schedules, are disorganized, forgetful, and sloppy.

**EXTRAVERSION** (assertive vs. reserved)
People who are often perceived as dominant, talkative, and full of energy have high extraversion scores. They tend to be enthusiastic, optimistic, sociable, and action-oriented individuals. They may appear more dominant in communication, as opposed to introverted people, who are rather

reserved in social situations (but not unfriendly or antisocial). Introverts tend to be quiet, reserved, task-oriented, and seem shy. They need less stimulation, and more time alone (just for themselves) than extraverts. Generally, people are combinations of extraversion and introversion traits.

**AGREEABLENESS** (cooperative vs. selfish)
Agreeable individuals are generally considerate, kind, generous, trustful, and friendly. They are affectionate and willing to help others. Disagreeable individuals place self-interest above getting along with others. They do not show interest in other people's feelings and concern for other people problems. They tend to be selfish, manipulative, rude, competitive and distrustful.

**NEUROTICISM** (nervous vs. calm)
Those who score high in neuroticism are very emotional, moody, tense, and insecure. They are more likely to interpret ordinary situations as threatening, and usually worry about a lot of things. They tend to have problems with emotional regulation and become stressed and upset easily. On the other hand, people with low scores in neuroticism tend to be calm, relaxed, secure, self-confident, and emotionally stable.

*"Do not compare, do not measure yourself against others.*
*No other way is like yours. All other ways deceive*
*and tempt you. You must fulfill the*
*way that is in you."*
(Carl Jung)

**Reflective questions:**

How would you describe yourself as a person?

What are the personality traits that you are more satisfied with? Which one would you like to change if you could?

Do you find yourself to be a more extraverted or introverted person?

Which traits do you value the most in other people?

Can you recognize some of the personality traits (described above) in coaches, players, and your peers?

## CULTURAL ISSUES

There is growing evidence that people in diverse countries, using very different languages, view individual differences in personality traits in ways similar to the Big Five. Some personality traits are apparently unique to individual countries. The importance of traits and the ways in which they are expressed can vary from culture to culture, as well as within the same culture over time. The universality of some traits suggests a biological basis in terms of genes and evolution, that they are part of what we call human nature. Differences in the ways in which traits are expressed and the uniqueness of some traits to specific cultures suggest that culture has an important role in facilitating adaptation to specific environments (Cervone and Pervin, 2013).

Many researchers have noted that the Big Five factors and their traits appear universally, as those traits have been found in more than 50 countries and diverse nations all over the world. Although the same factors are common to many cultures, major differences have been recognized in their relative importance and social desirability (Schultz and Schultz, 2009).

EXAMPLE: *In some countries extraversion and agreeableness tend to be more desirable than in others, but in other countries it is socially preferable to be more conscientious and emotionally stable than to be extraverted or open-minded.*

In addition, understanding all these findings in cultural diversity with respect to socially preferable traits, it is important not to be judgmental toward certain personalities you recognize in your domestic environment. Usually, many people define personality in terms of social attractiveness. A person with a "good personality" is one who impresses others with their ability to get along well with people (Ryckman, 2008). Defining personality in terms of social attractiveness is inadequate because it considers only 'attractive' aspects of personality, and implies that some people (with obviously unique personality traits) lack qualities.

EXAMPLE: *You may find a person who is really friendly, energetic, outgoing, but not reliable when it comes to time schedules and less open to new ideas. You would probably not want to work with this person on some important project. On the other hand, you may find a person with a very analytical style of thinking, sometimes even shy, but with a great sense of responsibility when it comes to work demands or deadlines. You would probably choose this person for collaboration on some projects.*

When thinking about personality, it is important not to consider it as a 'black or white' construct, but rather as a colorful, lively form. Also, in a sports environment we can find more extraverted personality traits and find them to be more preferable by coaches, spectators, fans, but, nevertheless, introverts in sports can be highly productive, successful and valuable individuals.

**Reflective questions:**

Do you recognize cultural differences in preferable traits over less preferable ones?

Do you think understanding these differences is important for you as a referee (especially if you are an international one)? How could these findings benefit you when preparing for international tournaments?

Do you usually perceive personalities in terms of social attractiveness or rather as a more complex construct with many characteristics?

How can this finding help you understand yourself and others better in your everyday life and officiating?

# PERSONAL CONSTRUCT THEORY

Proposed by psychologist George Kelly, the personal construct theory of personality (1955) describes personality in terms of cognitive processes. According to him, each person creates a set of cognitive constructs about environment – the ways of perceiving, explaining, interpreting, or construing events.

Each person has a unique way of looking at life that guides their behavior and predicts the behavior of other people. Based on those constructs or patterns, we make predictions about the future to formulate our responses and guide our actions. Therefore, to understand personality, we must first understand our cognitive constructs about the world, the patterns we use to interpret events.

# EXPLANATORY STYLE: OPTIMISTIC vs PESSIMISTIC

How you interpret or explain negative and positive events depends largely on your 'explanatory style'. Explanatory style is a habitual way of explaining events that stems directly from your view of your place in the world, whether you think you are valuable and deserving, or worthless and hopeless. It reveals whether you are an optimist or a pessimist (Seligman, 1990). Psychologist Martin Seligman in his book *Learned Optimism* (1990; 2006) described the main dimensions of optimistic and pessimistic explanatory styles: permanence, pervasiveness, and personalization.

**PERMANENCE: temporary vs. permanent**

People who are pessimists and give up easily believe the causes of bad events (that happen to them) are permanent, will persist, and will always be there to affect their lives, reflected in statements such as *"He never talks to me"* or *"I am not good at remembering dates"*.
People who explain bad events as temporary conditions have an optimistic style, reflected in statements such as *"I forgot his birthday because I was too busy that day."*

Optimistic people explain good events to themselves in terms of permanent causes: traits, abilities, always's, as in: *"I am talented and this is why I have succeeded."* Pessimists name temporary causes, such as moods, lack, or sometimes's, as in: *"It was a stroke of luck that day."*

People who believe good events have permanent causes try even harder after they succeed. People who see temporary reasons for good events may give up even when they succeed, believing success was a lucky coincidence.

**PERVASIVENESS: specific vs. universal**

People who make *universal* explanations for troubles give up on everything when failure strikes in one area. They tend to break under pressure, both for a long time and across situations, reflected in statements such as: "*All teachers are unfair.*"

People who make specific explanations may become helpless in that one part of their lives but remain generally strong through life, reflected in statements such as: "*That math professor is unfair.*"

The optimistic explanatory style for good events is opposite for bad events. The optimist believes that bad events have specific causes, while good events will enhance everything they do, as in: "*I am generally a very charming person.*"

The pessimist believes that bad events have universal causes, and that good events are caused by specific factors, as in: "*Because of my friends, she found me charming.*"

**PERSONALIZATION: internal vs. external**

When bad things happen, we can blame ourselves (internalize) or we can blame other people or circumstances (externalize). People who blame themselves when they fail have low self-esteem as a consequence. An example is the statement: "*I am not talented, and this is why I did not succeed.*" Low self-esteem usually comes from people using internal style for bad events. They think they are worthless, talentless, and unlovable. People who blame external events do not lose self-esteem when bad events strike. An example of this is: "*The coach had not explained it to me well, and this is why I did not improve.*"

The optimistic style of explaining good events is the opposite to the one used for bad events: it is internal rather than external. People who believe they cause good things tend to like themselves better than people who believe good things come from other people or circumstances.

According to Seligman (1990; 2006), personalization only controls how you feel about yourself, but pervasiveness and permanence the more important dimensions control what you do: *how long you are helpless and across how many situations*.

Seligman states that people can learn to become more optimistic by challenging their negative self-talk and replacing pessimistic thoughts with more positive and productive ones (1990; 2006). Even if pessimism is partially hereditary, it is also learned through childhood experiences and thinking habits developed through life. If people learn to become hopeless and pessimistic, they can learn to become more optimistic and happier.

## SELF-ACTUALIZATION THEORY OF PERSONALITY

Although much of our personality and behavior is determined by heredity, upbringing, and environment, psychologist Carl Rogers (1961, 1980) believed that we have within ourselves the capacity to choose and to become self-directed. He felt that individuals can play an active role in shaping their own lives and have the power to change. Like his colleague Abraham Maslow, he believed that we all have a drive toward personal growth and self-actualization. People are motivated by an innate tendency to develop their abilities and fulfill their potentials through self-actualization (Rogers, 1961, 1980). To actualize, maintain, and enhance the self is an important drive for all people.

*"Self-actualization is a journey,*
*not a destination."*
(Carl Rogers)

Like Albert Ellis, he accepts that everyone perceives situations differently, therefore, to understand an individual, we have to try to understand how they see the world. Rogers points out that how we perceive a situation depends on our mood, the type of person we are, our beliefs, and our past experiences. Our early experiences have some influence on personality development, but experiences later in life have a greater impact. Our present feelings are more vital to our personality then the events of our childhood.

Our self-concept is socially constructed. We tend to judge ourselves according to what others think of us rather than on what we feel. We behave in this way because of our high need for positive regard. This may result in us relying more on other people's judgements about our personal growth than on our own views.

For Rogers (1961, 1980), a healthy self-concept or personality is not a fixed identity but an identity open to possibilities and changes. The ultimate and necessary goal of life is to become a fully functioning person. As we live in an environment of constant change, we should be open to things that occur, and allow our fullest abilities to function, and in turn we can get the greatest satisfaction from our experiences.

According to him, the fully functioning person is/has:

- open to experiences
- able to perceive the world realistically
- the ability to live fully in the present moment
- trust in oneself
- sense of freedom, spontaneity, and creativity
- accepts responsibility for own actions and behavior
- treat others with positive regard

*"Growth occurs when individuals confront problems, struggle to master them, and through that struggle develop new aspects of their skills, capacities, views about life."*
(Carl Rogers)

# A final note

I hope that by reading this book you have gained some insight into the basic psychological principles and human nature and that this information will help you to better understand emotional reactions, behavior, and all the motivation behind them, especially when it comes to yourself and all the participants in a competitive environment such as sport. I truly believe that you will search for extra knowledge to become better educated in this important part of officiating – psychology and human nature. This knowledge can be very beneficial for you off and on the court.

For your future development in that direction, my knowledge, experience, and ideas are at your disposal.

# References

Ashton, M.C. (2018). *Individual differences and personality.* (3rd ed.) Cambridge, MA: Academic Press

Bandura, A. and Jeffrey, R. W. (1973). Role of symbolic coding and rehearsal processes in observational learning. *Journal of Personality and Social Psychology, 26,* 122 – 130.

Bandura, A. (1977). *Social learning theory.* Englewood Cliffs, NJ: Prentice-Hall.

Cervone, D. and Pervin, L.A. (2013). *Personality: Theory and research.* (12th ed.) Hoboken, NJ: Wiley & Sons

Cloninger, S.C. (2004). *Theories of personality: Understanding persons.* (4th ed.) New Jersey, NY: Pearson Prentice Hall.

Collin, C., Benson, N., Ginsburg, J., Grand, V., Lazyan, M., and Weeks, M. (2012). *The psychology book: Big ideas simply explained.* New York, NY: DK Publishing

Costa, P.T., Jr. and McCrae, R.R. (1985). *The NEO Personality Inventory manual.* Odessa, FL: Psychological Assessment Resources.

Costa, P.T., Jr. and McCrae, R.R. (1992). *NEO-PI-R: professional manual.* Odessa, FL: Psychological Assessment Resources.

Deckers, L. (2018). *Motivation: Biological, psychological, and environmental.* (5th ed.) New York, NY: Routledge.

Ekman, P. (1992). *Telling lies. Clues to deceit in the marketplace, politics, and marriage.* New York, NY: Norton & Company

Ekman, P. (2003). *Emotions revealed. Recognizing faces and feelings to improve communication and emotional life.* New York, NY: Times Books

Ekman, P. And Freisen, W.V. (2003). *Unmasking the face. A guide to recognizing emotions from facial expressions.* Cambridge, MA: Malor Books

Ellis, A. (1995). Changing Rational-Emotive Therapy (RET) to Rational Emotive Behavior Therapy (REBT). *Journal of Rational-Emotive & Cognitive-Behavior Therapy, Vol.13,* No. 2, 85 – 89.

Ellis, A. (2003). Early theories and practices of Rational Emotive Behavior Therapy and how they have been augmented and revised during the last three decades. *Journal of Rational-Emotive & Cognitive-Behavior Therapy, 21* (3/4), 219 – 243.

Erikson, E. (1950). *Childhood and society.* New York: W.W. Norton

Erikson, E.H. and Erikson, J.M. (1998). *The life cycle completed: Extended version.* New York: W.W. Norton

Eysenck, H.J. (1947). *Dimensions of personality.* London: K.Paul, Trench, Trubner & Co.

Eysenck, H.J. (1981). *A model of personality.* Berlin: Springer – Verlag

Eysenck, H.J. and Eysenck, M.W. (1985). *Personality and individual differences: A natural science approach.* New York: Plenum Press.

Feist, J. and Feist.G.J. (2008). *Theories of personality.* (7th ed.) New York,

NY: McGraw-Hill

Freud, S. (1960). *The Ego and the Id.* New York, NY: W.W. Norton & Company

Freud, A. (1993). *The ego and the mechanisms of defense.* London, UK: Karnac Books

Frijida, N. H. (2006) *The Laws of Emotion.* New York, NY: Routledge

Goleman, D. (1998). *Working with emotional intelligence.* New York: Bantam.

Goleman, D. (2000). *Leadership that gets result.* Boston, MA: Harvard Business Review Press

Goleman, D. (2009). *Emotional intelligence. Why it can matter more than IQ.* London: Bloomsbury Publishing.

Hull, C.L. (1943). *Principles of behavior.* New York, NY: Appleton-Century-Crofts.

Kasschau, R. A. (2003). *Understanding psychology.* Columbus, OH: McGraw-Hill

Kelly, G.A. (1955). *The psychology of personal constructs.* New York: Norton

Kenrick, D.T., Griskevicius, V., Neuberg, S.L., and Schaller, M. (2010). Renovating the pyramid of needs: Contemporary extensions built upon ancient foundations. *Perspective on Psychological Science, 5,* 292 – 314.

Maslow, A.H. (1943). A theory of human motivation. *Psychological Review, 50,* 370 – 396.

Martin, G. and Pear, J. (2015). *Behavior modification. What it is and how to do it?* New York, NY: Pearson

Mayer, J.D. and Salovey, P. (1997). What is emotional intelligence? In P. Salovey and D. Sluyter (ed.). *Emotional development and Emotional intelligence: Implications for educators.* New York, NY: Basic Book

McClelland, D. (1961). *The achieving society.* New Jersey: D. Van Nostrad Company

Mischel, W. (1996). *Personality and Assessment.* Mahwah, NJ: Lawrence Erlbaum Associates

Mischel, W., Shoda, Y. and Ayduk, O. (2008). *Introduction to Personality. Toward an integrative science of the person.* (8th ed.) Hoboken, NJ: John Wiley & Sons.

Musek, J. (2005). *Predmet, metode in področja psihologije.* Ljubljana: Oddelek za psihologijo, FFUL

Pervin, L.A. (2003). *The science of personality.* (2nd ed.) New York, NY: Oxford University Press

Plutchik, R. (2001). The nature of emotions. *American Scientist, Vol. 89,* No. 4, 344 – 350.

Ramnerö, J. And Törneke, N. (2008). *The ABC's of human behavior. Behavioral principles for the practicing clinician.* Oakland, CA: New Harbinger Publications.

Reeve, J. (2009). *Understanding Motivation and Emotion.* (5th ed.) Hoboken, NJ: Wiley.

Robinson, D.L. (2009). Brain function, emotional experience and personality. *Netherland Journal of Psychology, 64,* 152 – 167.

Rogers, C.R. (1961). *On becoming a person: A therapist's view of psychotherapy.* Boston: Houghton Miffin.

Rogers, C.R. (1980). *A way of being.* Boston: Houghton Miffin.

Ryan, R.M. and Deci, E.L. (2000). Intrinsic and extrinsic motivations: Classic definitions and new directions. *Contemporary Educational Psychology, 25,* 54 – 67.

Ryckman, R.M. (2008). *Theories of personality.* (9th ed.). Belmont, CA: Thompson Wadsworth

Salovey, P. and Caruso, D.R. (2004). *The emotionally intelligent manager: How to develop and use four key emotional skills for leadership.* San Francisco, CA: Jossey-Bass

Schultz D. P. and Schultz, S.E. (2009). *Theories of personality.* (9th ed.) Belmont, CA: Wadsworth

Schultz, D. P. and Schultz, S.E. (2013). *Theories of personality.* (10th ed.) Belmont, CA: Wadsworth

Seligman, M. (1990). *Learned optimism. How to change your mind and your life.* New York: Random House

Seligman, M. (2006). *Learned optimism. How to change your mind and your life.* (3rd ed.) New York: Vintage Books

Skinner, B. F. (1953). *Science and human behavior.* New York: Macmillan

Suri, and Gross, J.J. (2016). Emotion regulation: A valuation perspective. In L.F., Barrett, M. Lewis, and J. Jones-Haviland, (ed.) *Handbook of emotions.* (4th ed.) (pp. 453 – 466). New York, NY: Guilford Press

Winter, D.G. (1973). *The power motive.* New York: Free Press.

Zimmerman, B. J. (2000). Attaining self-regulation: A social cognitive perspective. In M. Boekaerts, P.R. Pintrich and M. Zeidner (Ed.) *Handbook of self-regulation* (pp.13 – 39). San Diego, CA: Academic Press.

# About the author

Dubravka Martinović is a sports psychologist from Croatia, also working internationally. She works with basketball, handball, football referees through individual consultations, seminars, and mental preparation programs. Since 2014, she has collaborated with FIBA as an associate for their referee departments, attending their clinics, seminars, and seasonal events, as part of their preparation programs. She is the author of the Manual for Basketball Referees' Mental Preparation, written exclusively for FIBA referees in 2016.